A consumer writer for 25 years, **Malcolm Stacey** began his journalistic career selling newspapers as a schoolboy on Doncaster racecourse. Since then he's contributed to all our national newspapers and has made more than 6,000 radio and TV programmes. Specializing in medical matters, he is perhaps best known for his investigative reports on Radio Four's *You and Yours* programme. *Atishoo!* is his third book.

All You'll Ever Need to Know
About the Common Cold

Malcolm Stacey

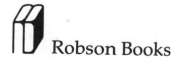

Robson Books

To Josephine

First published in Great Britain in 1993 by Robson Books Ltd, Bolsover House, 5–6 Clipstone Street, London W1P 7EB

Copyright © 1993 by Malcolm Stacey

British Library Cataloguing in Publication Data
A catalogue record for this title is available from the British Library

ISBN 0 86051 879 5

Photoset in North Wales by
Derek Doyle & Associates, Mold, Clwyd
Printed and bound in Great Britain by
Butler & Tanner Ltd, Frome and London

Contents

Contents

Acknowledgements

Thanks to Jo Perkins, Robin Thomas, Alice Moulding, Doug Waring, Richard Frederiks, Cathy Fletcher, Daniel Jodey-Michaels, Leslie Watts, Barney Wordsworth, John Howard, Debbie Higgins, David Berry, Shirley Cummings, Cyril and Joan Mitchell, Sherrie Desorde, Marjorie Freemantle, Ray Tiffany, Ian Dick, Nance Parry, Ellis Widdup, John Peel, John Dymock, James Watt, Phil Peel, Pat Plant, Lesley Caley, John Andrews, Ken Donnelly and Karen Mousley.

Preface

I once read a science fiction story in which the twist in the tale was, it seemed to me, far more horrific than any work by Edgar Allan Poe or Bram Stoker. A scientist experiments on himself to find an antidote for viruses – and accidentally gives himself an everlasting cold.

As a life-long sufferer from at least five colds a year I tremble at the thought of just how horrible this fate would be. We all hate colds, and I've always imagined hell not as a giant furnace but as a place where you catch a new cold every week.

Colds are a menace to us all. And unless you know your enemies and their weaknesses you can't retaliate. In this book you'll learn all you need to know about colds. Then you can fight back – and win.

Introduction

Colds are not only the world's most common illness, there are more of them every year than all other complaints combined. Britons suffer around 200 million colds a year, and people in the United States three times that number. The cost to commerce and industry is astronomical. The price of research into a cure is countless millions of pounds. And all over the world this damnable complaint is a source of discomfort and misery.

The sensation of a cold is familiar but difficult to describe. It's not a pain or a definite feeling like nausea. It doesn't immobilize you like a broken leg. True, the nose blocks up, making it difficult to breathe. But for most of a cold's duration, there are no breathing difficulties. The characteristic sore throat is not particularly painful.

The real misery of a cold is less tangible than that of other maladies. It's the general feeling of sheer unpleasantness which takes the joy out of special occasions and humdrum existence alike. It makes us feel fragile and unsociable as well as downright unwell. And on top of this general unwell feeling there is a sore throat, a headache, a fever, a runny nose, a cough, and a disappearing voice – all very nasty symptoms to put up with, especially all in one week.

More worryingly, colds often set off more serious conditions, including pneumonia, asthma, tuberculosis, and meningitis; and they can cause inflammation around the heart.

Why then is the cold often described as a mild illness? H.G.

Wells referred to the cold as 'humble'. The writers of most home medical guides feel it's not worth spending time on. A typical entry might be:

> An infection of the upper respiratory tract caused by viruses. There is no cure for a cold, which usually comes to an end within a week.

Family doctors have told me that the cold isn't part of their training; and that questions about it are never asked in the exam room. All very dismissive. And yet we all know that the depressing symptoms often drag on for more than a week. Furthermore, though scientific progress towards a total cure is painfully slow, we are not nearly so powerless against colds as some doctors seem to think.

There are a host of steps you can take to shorten, ease and even prevent the symptoms. Contrary to popular belief, most of these ways have scientific credentials. All the effective cures and preventatives are detailed in this book – as are some of the more ludicrous treatments that have been hallowed by tradition or favoured by quacks. My research has been spurred on by personal reasons. Perhaps because of my job as an investigative journalist, meeting many different people and working odd hours, I have suffered more colds than average. During some years there have been wall-to-wall episodes all winter. My grandfather met his death after a cold affected his chest. My mother, who suffered from emphysema, also died probably after a cold aggravated her condition.

But since researching this book, my own number of attacks has dropped from five or six a year to two, and the colds I still get don't last as long as they used to. I now try all the cures approved by bona fide researchers into the disease, and I have discarded many useless remedies I once had faith in.

I hope this guide will be of equal help to you. I think it will.

What Is a Cold?

If your doctor tells you 'I think you have acute coryza', don't panic – he's only using the medical term for the common cold. (If you want to chide him for needless use of technical language, your reply should be, 'Oh, you mean acute nasopharyngitis' – which is another medical name for this complaint.)

Strictly speaking, there's no such thing as a 'cold in the nose'. Coryza is a disease of the entire upper respiratory tract, which consists not only of the many tubes and cavities inside your nose, but also a few passages just below it and the top half of your throat. Diseases other than coryza can affect the upper respiratory tract. They include laryngitis, tonsillitis and influenza, together with some familiar childhood maladies like measles and whooping cough.

Coryza is caused not by bacteria, like some of the complaints above, but by a virus. (The difference between these two types of microscopic organisms is explained in the next chapter). The viruses which invade our bodies always home in on a specific part. The polio virus, for instance, attacks the spinal cord, mumps the salivary glands, hepatitis the liver, AIDS the immune system and so on. A cold virus attacks the nose, some of the sinuses and the upper part of the throat.

What Kind of Virus?

At least 200 different types of cold virus have been identified

1

It's acute Nasopharyngitis, actually

and it's likely that at least another 100 remain to be discovered. Even more alarming is the probability that existing varieties are mutating (changing genetically) to form even more types. This is hard to prove because it's not known if the viruses still being unmasked are hitherto undiscovered species which have been around a long time or are previously known varieties which have changed form. If cold viruses are constantly evolving – and flu viruses certainly do – the outlook is bleak. We'll get even more sniffles in the future.

There are several different groups of cold virus, but the most common are the rhinoviruses, from the Greek word *rhinon* ('nose'). There are 113 known forms of rhinovirus and they cause two out of every five colds.

Cold bugs are parasites. They attach themselves to healthy cells which, ever hungry for protein, swallow them up. Once inside they metaphorically shout 'Feed me!'

I mentioned that cold-causing viruses attack the upper respiratory system. Their point of entry into the system is the mucous membrane. This lines the micro-tubes and mini-caverns inside the nose. It's made up of layers of cells which produce a thin, transparent liquid called mucus. 'Coryza' that term used by your doctor, comes from the Greek word for nasal mucus. The membrane is covered in very fine hairs that constantly wave like grass in a breeze – but always in one direction. The hairs move the mucus along the nasal passages. When tiny foreign bodies – bacteria, say, or pollen, pepper, or bits of feather land at the nose's entrance, a complex security system gets going. Its job is to prevent dust and germs finding their way into the lungs, where they could wreak havoc on some very sensitive tissues. Larger particles get no further than the larger hairs in your nostrils. It's because of their job as 'bouncers' that you shouldn't over-trim these hairs just to improve your appearance.

Smaller foreign bodies – including living organisms – which successfully negotiate this first obstacle get stuck to the magic carpet of mucus. With the aid of the cells' moving hairs, this carpet carries its unwanted burden away from the lungs and down the gullet out of harm's way.

With all that rubbish trapped in the nasal secretions, like weed in the Sargasso Sea, it's no wonder the cells which produce the mucus are vulnerable to infection. Cold viruses are tiny enough to find their way through the mucus and to latch onto the cells which manufacture it in the membrane. This action eventually destroys the cells – and produces all those misery-making symptoms we recognize as a cold.

But there's worse to come. Once the viruses have weakened the cell walls, larger germs such as bacteria, previously ineffective against the mucous membrane, may join the fray. And by now the damaged tissue is in no state to resist. These opportunistic bacteria often cause complications more serious than the original cold.

Most colds last for a week. A few vanish overnight; even fewer survive a fortnight. If you're still snuffling after two weeks, there are two possibilities. You have either: caught another cold (two or more different viruses can invade the nose at the same time) or you have been assailed by harmful bacteria which have taken hold after the cold virus has done its work.

Antibiotics – No Cure for Colds

While bacteria can be polished off by antibiotics, viruses are, with very rare exceptions, quite impervious to them. You often hear it said, 'I've had a nasty cold, but it didn't last long once my doctor gave me antibiotics.' A GP will indeed prescribe antibiotics for cold symptoms, but only if he thinks bacteria may be taking advantage of damage previously done by cold viruses.

How Many Colds a Year?

Household medical books tell us that a fairly healthy adult can expect three colds a year. In fact, the true average is nearer six, and it's not exceptional to have 10.

Babies and toddlers, with immature immunity systems,

will get up to a dozen a year, while elderly people with the advantage of a lifetime's experience of fending off viruses will get two. On the other hand, children shrug colds off quickly, whereas among old people each cold lasts longer than average.

Many people claim they never catch a cold. Most are simply boasting, but for some it is the literal truth. Scientific surveys show that 8 out of 100 people never catch a cold at all. One volunteer attended the Common Cold Research Centre no fewer than 24 times. Only once did he produce cold symptoms – and they were hardly noticeable.

It may be that non-sufferers have extra robust immunity systems. This could be the gift of heredity, or possibly the result of a healthy diet. In any event, there's no doubt that if the ratio of cold-free people to cold-prone people could be increased by wiser eating habits, fewer colds would be caught and the scourge would diminish.

How Colds Begin

When someone with a cold sneezes, he or she discharges anything from 100,000 to a million infected droplets into the air. Each droplet will be crammed with cold viruses. If you are near the sneezer the best tip is to open your mouth and temporarily breathe through that. You may look rather gormless, but viruses paddling up your nose are more likely to give you a cold than those sucked through the lips.

Research suggests that the mouth isn't particularly hospitable to viruses. Most people would say that kissing someone with the sniffles is asking for trouble, but in fact you are not likely to catch a cold this way. And although drinking from a glass or cup which may still have traces of infected saliva from somebody else on the rim may not be a delightful thought, it probably won't give you a cold.

Although their main entry point is through the nose, cold viruses have another handy portal – the tear ducts. If infected droplets from someone's cough or sneeze get on your hand and you rub your eyes in the next hour or two, a cold is the

*The best tip is to open your mouth
and temporarily breathe through that*

probable result. The virus can also invade your body by touch. If a cold patient blows his nose and some of his cold viruses move from his handkerchief to his hand, they will stay there for some time. Now, if you were to shake his hand, his bugs would transfer to your fingers. All you have to do now is absent-mindedly finger your face – and you'd better buy some aspirin and a nasal spray.

The truth is that cold viruses are all over the place: in the air, in the dust, on all sorts of surfaces and on sticky fingers everywhere.

When Are Colds Most Infectious?

Experts differ on this, but most agree the risks are greater at the beginning, when viruses have yet to encounter and be weakened by antibodies – the proteins produced by our immune system to attack foreign organisms that invade the body. On the other hand, a patient in the early stages of a cold will be harbouring comparatively few viruses, because they will not have had time to multiply. So some virologists believe that the viruses are most likely to emigrate towards the end of a cold. In which case, you are just as likely to catch a cold if you associate with a victim who's over the worst.

Field trials have tended to show, however, that colds are most infectious as soon as symptoms appear, and in fact may even reach a peak of infectiousness during the incubation period immediately before that. So if you magnanimously decide to stay at home from work or college to protect your colleagues and friends, you may be wasting your time – it may already be too late.

Cold Virus – the Ultimate Parasite

A virus, the villain of the piece, is a tiny organism made up of a remarkable substance called nucleic acid surrounded by protein. It's in the form of a spiral, and is so small it makes even microscopic bacteria look like monsters. And most cold organisms are among the smallest viruses known.

There's been a lot of scientific discussion as to whether viruses are really life forms at all. They are quite different from all other forms of life, and yet anything with such an aggressive drive to reproduce itself must surely be alive.

Bacteria, some of which also cause diseases of the upper respiratory tract, are much more like plants or animals than viruses are. Bacteria are single-cell entities which absorb food until they are big enough to divide into two. This is also what the billions of cells which make up a plant or animal do. In this way our bodies are constantly renewed.

Bacteria, which come in at least 1500 known varieties, can be found almost anywhere. But if we only had to fend off the infections and illnesses caused by bacteria, life would be much easier. Most of them can be trounced by antibiotics such as penicillin. Viruses, on the other hand, laugh at antibiotics.

A cold virus is a parasite – an organism that is able to absorb food and reproduce itself only by attaching itself to another organism. Most parasites are highly selective about the host organism on which they depend. Cold viruses, for instance, cannot survive merely by alighting on any part of your body. They are incapable of moving themselves, so they will survive and multiply only if, by some chance, they are blown, or are deposited, onto the mucus in our nose or upper throat.

The Viral Invasion

The viruses can get to these target sites in a variety of ways. You may, for instance, unwittingly breathe in air that has become virus-rich as a result of a cold victim sneezing nearby. Or you might shake that person's hand and later rub your nose.

What happens next is a bit of a horror story.

Step 1. The protein in the virus attaches itself to the cell. Automatically, the cell 'swallows' the intruder, and the nucleic acid of the virus sets up shop inside.

Step 2. A living cell is a miniature chemical factory, making all the ingredients necessary for the production of new cells. The virus's nucleic acid takes over the cell, instructing it to produce nucleic acid and the protein needed to enclose it. In other words, the cell is converted into a virus production plant.

Step 3. The cell is eventually exhausted and dies, whereupon the multitude of new viruses it produced look for fresh cells to colonize.

Step 4. The body's response to this destructive pandemonium in the cells is to increase production of mucus in order to wash away the invading viruses. All this mucus becomes overloaded with new viruses, which infect more and more cells as the mucus drains down the throat. Soon all the nose and upper throat are under attack and you display the usual symptoms of a heavy cold.

Step 5. Your coughs and sneezes expel droplets of mucus crammed with viruses into the atmosphere, where others may breathe them in – and the cycle begins anew.

Counter-attack

It's easy to see how all this cell destruction would, if allowed to continue indefinitely, lead to serious damage to the nose. Luckily the body has its own defence to deal with the threat. This is what's known as our immune system. The chief item in its armoury are glands which manufacture antibodies – special proteins which are automatically produced when foreign substances enter the body and have the ability to neutralize them. Eventually the spent antibodies together with dead cells get mixed up with the colourless nasal discharge and thicken it – a sure sign that you are over the worst of your cold.

Antibodies are a crucial part of the body's defence against infections of every kind. Our first line of defence is the skin. Obviously, an unbroken skin surface provides an effective barrier against disease. But it so happens that cold viruses cannot infect us even through cuts, sores, boils, spots or other temporary gaps in this defensive layer. On the other hand, the eyes and linings of the nose and throat are more open to attack, and although they contain natural disinfectants, these are more effective against bacteria than viruses.

We can summarize the body's total response to an onslaught by cold viruses in the following way: sentries, in the form of chemicals activated by the virus invasion, tell the brain what's happening, whereupon the body's defence system despatches extra supplies of blood to the spot where the viruses have established a beachhead. This causes tissues in the nose and throat to swell and inflame, bringing on a blocked nose and a raspy throat. At the same time – and partly due to the expense of energy involved in the body's response – our defence system raises our temperature. The effect of this is to inhibit the spread of viruses or to stimulate more antibodies, or probably both.

A key role in the cold war is played by the lymph system. The lymph system and the bone marrow each make different types of white blood cells, which are the foot soldiers in the body's war against infection. As soon as foreign substances attack the body, production of white blood cells increases rapidly, and these are conveyed via the lymph system and the blood circulatory system to the infected area.

Antibodies are white cells that are, you might say, tailor-made to deal with the particular infection involved. In the case of a cold, the antibodies enclose and coat the cold viruses, so isolating them from the body's living cells. This effectively defeats the invasion because, as we have seen, it is only by colonizing and being fed by living cells that the cold viruses can reproduce. Eventually, the viruses and white blood cells are destroyed and expelled in the mucus, which changes from a thin, transparent liquid to thickish green stuff. Once the mucus changes colour you can take heart that the struggle is almost over.

Some white blood cells have a memory. They can store the details of each virus that causes trouble. If such a virus invades the body again, these cells quickly mobilize the right kind of antibody to neutralize it. So our natural immunity to viruses gradually increases and we suffer from fewer viral illnesses as we get older.

Vaccination and Colds

This is how vaccination works. A few living or dead viruses causing a specific disease are put into the bloodstream in sufficient quantities to cause a mild attack. Antibodies, quickly manufactured by immunity cells, are mobilized to see off the viruses. The antibodies then remain in the system ready to do their duty again if a natural attack takes place later on. Some immune systems can continue to 'recognize' the structure of such inoculated viruses for up to 70 years. Viruses causing yellow fever are a case in point.

Vaccinations have been tried against the common cold, but the effect was so marginal, the results weren't worth the effort or expense. There are two reasons why anti-cold vaccines aren't up to the job. First, cold viruses don't enter the blood stream, which is where antibodies are most numerous. They only attack cells on the surface of the nose or throat. Second, we would need a different jab for each of the several hundred cold viruses so far identified.

As it happens, the situation may not be quite so bleak.

Some cold viruses are pretty much alike, and recent research suggests that a vaccine for one might also be effective against several others in the same 'family' of viruses. For the time being, however, our best defence is the natural immunity we develop over years of fighting a whole range of different cold viruses.

Why Antibiotics Can't Help

The mass production of penicillin in 1942, and the swift development of other antibiotics, caused a revolution in the struggle against diseases and infections that until then had killed countless millions of people. Smallpox, syphilis and tuberculosis were just three among many scourges that could be cured by antibiotics.

But then came disappointment. It was found that antibiotics did not neutralize viruses, which, as we've seen, attack our bodies in quite a different way from bacteria and other agents of infection.

There is, however, at least one cold-causing agent which can be cured by antibiotics. It's in a group called the mycoplasmas. Like true viruses, these organisms are tiny enough to pass through the laboratory filters which trap bacteria. They also lack the robust wall of a bacterial cell.

If you catch a cold from this bug you can, in theory, be quickly cured. In practice, by the time the cause of your sniffles has been identified, your cold will probably be over.

Killing the Cold Bugs

Cold viruses are not indestructible. In laboratory experiments, a number of chemical compounds have proved lethal to viruses which have been allowed to infect living human tissue. The only trouble with these germ killers is that they also attack the cells of human tissue.

There is one virus-immobilizer which doesn't harm human tissue. In fact, it's actually made by our cells. It's a protein called interferon, and a very small amount of this chemical is produced when cold viruses attack. Interferon is passed on to still-healthy neighbouring cells which are to help them protect themselves. The trouble is, the body never produces enough of the stuff to make much difference. (One reason why vitamin C is thought to help against colds is that it is believed to trigger the production of interferon.)

It's possible to extract interferon from animal tissue, but this is expensive. And a lot of the substance, if applied to virus-infected cells in the nose and throat, would be swept away by the tide of mucus. As well as these snags, interferon has been found to produce side effects that are not unlike those of the cold itself!

The Diary of a Simple Cold

This record is based on the timetable of a commonplace but persistent cold. If you enjoy good health and do not suffer from stress or over-tiredness, you are unlikely to experience all the symptoms described. And even if your vitality is low, you'd be unlucky to suffer all these effects from one viral attack.

However, it's worth charting this 'typical' dose to give you an idea of how far your affliction has progressed at a given moment and how many more days of misery you can expect to suffer.

Monday
AM You share a bus with a cold sufferer. Viruses from one of his sneezes land on the bell. You ring the bell to enable you to get off the bus. A little later, you unconsciously pull at your nose or rub your eyes.
PM The incubation period starts as viruses attack the lining of your nose. There are no immediate symptoms.

Tuesday
AM You feel more alert than usual, perhaps even cheerful. Alternatively, you might feel slightly depressed. In either case it is because extra blood is sent to the head in an early attempt to ward off the attack.

PM You notice a tight sensation inside your nose near the bridge, as though your nose was starting to grow. This feeling, slight at first, gets more oppressive later.

14

Evening. You feel chilly even in a warm room. (This is why the malady came to be known as a cold in the first place). This feeling, which causes the occasional shiver, is because blood is being diverted away from the skin to keep the inner body warmer. This is a typical manoeuvre by the body's natural thermostat to counter a viral invasion.

Towards bedtime you sneeze three or four times. There's slightly more tightening in your nose. Such early symptoms are so fleeting they often go unnoticed.

Wednesday
AM The glands under one or both ears have begun to fight the infection. They swell under the effort and ache, especially when you swallow. Also, they may slightly alter the shape of your face.

You wake up with a scratchy throat. Those still not sure they have a cold can regard this as the clincher. Sometimes there is a more localized pain further down the throat, often centred on one of your tonsils.

PM The sore throat gets more painful. The viruses multiply rapidly and move upwards into the nose. The brain sends blood to the besieged areas of the nose and throat, which become inflamed and swell the delicate linings.

Evening. You really know you're in trouble when a thin watery trickle starts in one nostril. You lose your appetite.

Thursday
AM You wake with a transparent discharge from both nostrils. Your eyes water and there is the beginning of a generalized headache. You can no longer detect delicate aromas, such as that of roses, because the scent glands in your nose are engulfed by the discharge.

PM You run a slight temperature of around 101°F and your joints and legs begin to ache. Your headache, often linked to a fever, begins to throb.

You can no longer detect delicate aromas

Evening. A general, indefinable, flu-ey feeling takes hold. This varies in severity: one minute you feel lousy, another almost normal. You shiver slightly when you go to the toilet.

Overnight. If you sleep on your side, the nostril nearer the pillow becomes blocked while the other one stays clear. This is because the mucus drains downwards. Turning over from time to time loosens it so that you can blow it clear.

Friday
AM The feverishness and the headache have gone. The limbs stop aching. The sore throat probably goes too. But you still feel poorly.
    The colourless discharge from your nose increases. This may be continuous, depending on the type of virus. If the discharge is severe, frequent blowing makes the skin around the nostrils sore and red.

PM Swollen blood vessels constrict your nasal passages and block both nostrils. You can no longer smell anything at all. You can't taste food properly either, because the olfactory glands, which govern your sense of smell, also play a major part in the ability to detect flavours.

Overnight. The discharge from your mucous membrane dripping down your throat will make you cough, keeping you awake. A hot drink eases it.

Saturday

AM The nose is by now totally blocked. It's harder to blow the discharge free as it thickens and changes to a yellowy-green colour.

PM The blockage continues. You may feel sick as thick mucus finds its way into your stomach. (Some people get nose bleeds at this stage, compounding the misery.)

Sunday
AM The discharge is now even thicker and greener. This is because it is teeming with white blood cells which have died in combat with the virus as well as bacteria from your nose. There may be tiny traces of red blood in the discharge, and it has a slightly sweet taste. As this thickened mucus gradually loosens it begins to migrate to your chest. But at least your chills and shivers disappear.

PM Your voice becomes hoarse, and although you generally feel a lot better, you get croakier in the evening.

Overnight. You sleep better because it's easier to breathe.

Monday
AM A persistent tickly cough develops. This is usually of the dry type, though it may bring up thick phlegm.

PM The voice may vanish altogether, especially if you use it a lot, and you become an object of mirth among family and friends.

Tuesday
Apart from coughing occasionally, and the appearance of phlegm, your cold symptoms have all but disappeared. The voice is back, but will sound hoarse for the rest of the day.

Wednesday
It's over at last! You can breathe through your nose again. But the phlegm in your throat remains and may need coughing up for another two weeks. It's also possible to suck this stuff up from your lower throat into the mouth.

Types of Cold

For some people colds run the same course every time. For example, they may get a scratchy throat for two days, a runny nose for four, after which they become gradually more blocked up and finish up with a cough and loss of voice.

Now this kind of fixed pattern is odd for an illness which is caused by any one of 300 or more different agents. The likely explanation is that these people's bodily defences react in the same way to all invasions of the nose and upper throat, whereas other people have defence systems which tailor their responses to different bugs.

No one in the medical world seems certain why there should be such differences in the behaviour of the defence system between individuals. It could be that the efficiency of our immunity set-up ebbs and flows depending on our diet, vitality or personal circumstances.

Although the symptoms may be identical and follow a similar chronological order in every cold an individual suffers, their severity may vary because some viruses are nastier than others.

Virologists grade colds according to severity. By looking at the following list, you'll be able to tell whether you have a stinker or merely a minor tickle. Then, when friends inquire after your health, at least you can bore them with a more accurate description than 'I feel pretty rotten' or 'Not too bad, thanks'.

I've also included the sort of treatment suitable for each type of cold. This is only a rough guide as it does not include the many effective treatments and traditional remedies explored elsewhere in this book.

Mini-Cold

The symptoms include the suggestion of a scratchy throat, two or three sneezes, and a tickle or tightness inside the nose. These don't get worse, however, and after a day or two you feel right as rain.

We probably catch many more mini-colds than we realize: they are so slight that often we are not aware of them. Records show that many boasters who claim they never have colds frequently have this minor complaint.

Action: You cannot tell at first if you are developing this kind of slight cold or one of its more serious cousins. So the moment early signs occur take a gram of Vitamin C every two hours and try to get an early night. With a bit of luck you will be your normal self in the morning.

Mild Cold

Occasional sneezing at first, then a dry sore throat followed after a day or two by a runny nose. You will probably need a fresh handkerchief twice a day. There are none of the oppressive symptoms like headache, high temperature or aches or pains. Sufferers feel better in three to five days.

Action: Keep a few handkerchiefs ready and keep topped up with vitamin C tablets or zinc preparations (see pages 51 and 55). Try to abort the cold with a drink or two of wine or beer per day. Sleep as much as you can, but do not cancel engagements. It's just about possible to put a cold as innocuous as this to the back of your mind.

Average Cold

This one lasts about a week. The nose runs more. Victims have a slight rise of temperature at first and may shiver and sweat from time to time. They certainly look as though they have a cold: they are constantly using their handkerchiefs and the area around the nostrils becomes sore.

The amount of mucus generated will probably cause wheeziness and coughing.

Action: As for a mild cold, but take aspirin or, preferably, paracetamol for headaches and any rise in temperature. Go to bed if you feel really lousy, but don't stay there too long as this can make you feel worse.

Heavy Cold

This is more like flu than a cold. In fact, even doctors can't always tell the difference, so they sometimes call them 'influenza colds' – a pretty meaningless term.

A really nasty cold comes with all the usual problems, only more so. You also have fever, headache, loss of appetite and a cough. And even if you want to go into work, you probably ache so much you can't.

Action: Go to bed and sleep as much as you can. Eat a lot, but keep off junk food. Don't worry if your appetite goes – the body can live on its fat reserves for some days without ill effect. Drink a lot of water, soup and fruit juice. This is specially important if you have a high temperature as a fever needs a lot of moisture. Avoid coffee and tea – the caffeine in them is a stimulant which won't help you to relax.

Maverick Colds

Some cold viruses cause fever, others don't. Some produce painfully sore throats, but don't cause the nose to run so much; others produce a Niagara Falls of a cold, but no other symptoms. In fact, up to 200 times the normal amount of mucus has been discovered flowing from some hapless patients.

If viruses do have a particular blueprint for their own stock of symptoms, those around you will know whom to blame if their cold develops on the same lines. But on those occasions when your partner develops completely different cold symptoms, it's likely that another brand of virus is having its wicked way.

And the danger then arises that he'll go on to catch your cold, and you'll succumb to his!

The Piggy-back Cold

As with most other illnesses, a cold sufferer can undergo a relapse. One moment you seem to be getting over the worst, and then without warning your nose resumes running with renewed fury, your throat becomes sore and you begin to feel fluey again.

A secondary complaint may be setting in, often as a result of the cold virus chipping away at nose and throat tissue, allowing bacteria to take advantage. This may lead to serious illnesses such as pneumonia or bronchitis. But more usually, when previously subsiding symptoms suddenly flare up again, it simply means another cold has set up shop. This sort of follow-up cold isn't unusual. And the second bout is sometimes worse than the first, or at least lasts longer, because the body and its defences have already been depleted by the original attack.

Cold-free Years

Another mystery is how, one year, we'll fall foul of a string of colds and then, all through the next, our noses and throats stay perfectly healthy. Yet we haven't changed home, our place of work, our diet or any other aspect of our life.

A remarkable explanation for this has been suggested by some research in the United States. It is known that undue stress, caused either by happy events like falling in love or miserable ones like being made redundant, helps colds to thrive. But the American research showed that this syndrome is more complicated than that. One group of volunteers was found to get more colds when there hadn't been any unusual happenings in their year at all. But further investigations showed that they had each had a particular exciting experience of some kind in the year *before*. And volunteers who hadn't experienced any such notable excitements in the previous year stayed cold-free.

Yet another indication that the common cold is among the great mysteries of the world!

Effective Cures

The crew of the space ship *Enterprise* get lots of peculiar afflictions in *Star Trek*, including (as I recall) becoming fighting mad, turning very childish, and galloping forwards to the age of 90 in a few minutes. But they never catch colds.

Back in the 20th century, because of difficulties already explained, we still can't prevent colds. And we still have no total cure – no short course of pills which will annihilate the viruses and spare us the usual succession of dreary symptoms.

Yet our failure (so far) to develop drugs that vanquish colds doesn't mean that there's nothing we can do about them. Elsewhere in this guide I detail dozens of ways to treat and limit an existing cold. They're all worth trying. At this point I just want to summarize some of the most effective responses to the symptoms.

The Easy Anti-cold Plan

* For headaches, a temperature or aching muscles and limbs, take aspirin or paracetamol. Ask for them specifically. There's little point in buying some expensive proprietary cold remedies, whose only useful ingredient may be one of these common pain-killers.
* Take 1 gram of vitamin C every four hours until the symptoms subside. By staggering the pills throughout the day you'll keep a constant supply in the blood.
* Take zinc. Zinc tablets can be expensive, but the mineral is

present in egg-yolks, milk and whole-grain cereals.
* Drink one pint of beer, one glass of spirits or two glasses of wine a day.
* If your nose blocks up, use a nasal spray – but sparingly.
* Inhale steam from a large bowl filled with water boiled in a kettle.
* Suck a boiled sweet for a sore throat.
* Keep warm. There's no evidence that chilling makes it easier to catch colds, but it will make symptoms worse.
* Drink plenty of fruit juice, preferably diluted with warmed water. Hot soup will also help to keep your nose and throat passages free.
* Avoid tobacco smoke, building dust and pollen. Don't disturb household dust by using the vaccum cleaner or shaking rugs. These irritants make all the symptoms harder to bear.
* Get as much sleep as you can.
* Stay off work – or at least slow down, so your body can concentrate energy in your natural defences.

How to Treat a Feverish Cold

The body will raise its temperature to fight colds. The extra heat is believed to slow the rate at which the virus multiplies. It may also encourage the growth of more antibodies. Thus a 'fever', which most of us regard as a problem, is actually very helpful.

The body's defence system has a natural 'thermostat' which controls our temperature. When it gets cold, this thermostat causes our blood vessels to constrict, allowing less heat to escape through the skin. When the temperature rises, the blood vessels open up and our sweat glands release moisture, which then evaporates and we feel cooler.

The body's thermostat is also activated by the presence of hostile substances. While the white blood cells are tackling the intruders, they release a chemical which is carried to the central nervous system – the body's communications centre. This alerts the thermostat, which closes bloodcells, raising

Sorry about this Vicar, he's been gargling again

the temperature.

High temperatures can be dangerous, but in the case of a cold they rarely rise above 38.5°C, or 101°F. Trying to reduce your temperature to its normal level is not always a good idea since it hinders your body's effort to overcome the viruses.

The best way to deal with a feverish cold is to go to bed. This keeps the body warm, so it wastes less energy in raising your internal temperature. Drink lots of water and fruit juices, as fevers deplete the body's fluid. You need to consume enough extra liquid to enable you to keep going to the toilet normally.

Temperatures in children rise higher than adults, which sometimes alarms parents. Fever in elderly people is less marked.

Easing a Sore Throat

This is an early sign of a cold – and usually the first of the irritations to disappear. If the soreness lasts more than a few days you may have a different kind of complaint set off by bacteria or a non-cold virus. This type of soreness isn't so much uncomfortable as downright painful.

Ease a sore throat by gargling with a teaspoon each of salt and bicarbonate of soda in a glass of water. Another useful mixture is two teaspoons of cider vinegar and two of honey in a cupful of warm water. Sip it slowly. Or have a bit more fun by gargling with neat whisky or rum. This should then be swallowed – in the interests of economy and a general feeling of wellbeing!

Treating a Headache Caused by a Cold

If your temples start throbbing in the first few days of infection, you can be sure your cold is going to be a stinker. A cold headache is difficult to pin down to one area, and it often throbs in time with the pulse. It's more unpleasant than its near relative which accompanies a hangover.

Fortunately a headache is one symptom of colds which can

be overcome by medicines. Aspirin or paracetamol should do the trick. Both these analgesics (the doctor's word for pain-killers) can be dangerous if taken in excess, so some doctors recommend that you alternate the tablets. So you might start with aspirin, taking the dosage recommended on the label. Then, when another dose is due, you take paracetamol instead – and so on. In this way you should not suffer side effects from either pain-killer.

Aspirin should not be given to children under twelve, as on very rare occasions it can lead to Reye's Syndrome, which may damage the brain and liver.

Treating a Cough Caused by a Cold

A cough is useful. The urge to cough signals the body's need to get rid of something that may threaten the delicate tissues of the lungs.

Coughing can signify anything from a serious illness such as tuberculosis to a speck of dust in the throat. During a cold, coughing is often triggered by nasal fluids dripping down the back of the throat. As it is a protective reaction, occasional coughing should not be suppressed. One of my school teachers, clearly in the interests of a quiet life rather than my health, once admonished me with the imbecile maxim: 'To cure a cough, don't cough'.

Sometimes, however, a cough can become troublesome, especially at night when you are trying to sleep. So here are a few tips for curbing a cough caused by a cold. (They're not necessarily all appropriate to problems caused by other complaints).
* Use pillows to prop up your head at night. This will ease the flow of irritating mucus dribbling down your throat.
* As soon as you start coughing in the small hours, reach for your hankie. If the stuff comes out of your nose, it can't run down your throat and do mischief in your lungs.
* Hot drinks soothe a cough by helping to shift any mucus lying around in the passages.
* Inhaling steam from a bowl of freshly boiled water will stop you hacking as well as unblock your nose (see page 24).

How to Avoid Colds

Whenever people are gathered together the air around them is likely to be heaving with infections. So how do most of us stay cold-free much of the time? And how do the lucky one in 10 of the population manage to avoid a runny nose year after year?

The answers to both questions lie in our body's defence system. If this is healthy we can hold the bugs at bay. In fact, many doctors believe that catching cold is the result of a brief interruption of our natural barrier against all kinds of virus. So it follows that a healthy immune system will keep the colds we suffer to a minimum, and could even eradicate them from our lives.

Giving Viruses the Slip

It's known that, once they've left their human host, cold viruses lurk about on all sorts of surfaces like fruit-machine handles, steering wheels, computer keyboards, and books and magazines. They can live outside a human body for at least an hour and sometimes as long as three, especially if the air is more damp than usual.

To catch a cold you not only have to touch a virus-infected area with your fingers, but then transfer the virus from your fingers to the entrance to your nose. It's no good insisting you never finger your nose – we all do. We also touch or rub our eyes a lot. This also suits the cold viruses, which can

breach the body's defences by entering through our
tear-ducts.

So when colds are going the rounds, a worthwhile
precaution is to wash our hands as often as possible. A
half-hearted splash around won't do – you must have a
proper surgeon's scrub with soap and water. It's also worth
occasionally wiping telephones, tables, kitchen tops and the
like with diluted bleaches, especially if you've had a
coughing and spluttering visitor.

There are, however, more subtle and longer-lasting ways
of keeping colds out of your life. These preventative methods
described below have been clinically 'proved'.

Put Those Worries Behind You!

You don't have to be a hypochondriac to worry about
catching a cold. It's quite natural to expect the worst when
you're just about to go on a scuba-diving holiday or be taken
down the aisle. Most of us nervously feel our throats and
make a few exploratory swallows if a little tickle comes on
when an important social or business event is imminent.

But experience tells us that merely fretting about the
possibility of a cold is enough to bring one on. Scientific
research seems to support this. Or, rather, research suggests
that a person in a happy, optimistic frame of mind fends off
infection better than a worrier. So the first trick is: never give
colds a second thought – at least until you're sure you've got
one.

Fit in Body, Fit in Nose

We've seen how our immune system fights viruses with
antibodies. Obviously, the more of these antibodies we can
produce at times of crisis the better, and it has been shown
that the fitter we are, the more (and stronger) antibodies will
we be able to produce. So a healthy diet is important.

Exercise will help too. But don't overdo it. Some experts
believe that, among fitness fanatics, too much of the body's

resources go into building muscles at the expense of its immunity system, which may become deprived of nutrients. This is one reason why professional sportsmen and women, especially runners and weightlifters, complain of more colds than average.

Dodging the Germs

A friend of mine insists he never gets a cold. He may simply be bragging, or he may have inherited a better than average set of immunity cells from his parents. He, however, maintains the trick is worked simply by avoiding people who're coughing and sneezing.

This is easier said than done. If the person sitting next to you on the train has obvious cold symptoms, such as a streaming nose, he or she will have passed the infectious stage. On the other hand the chap opposite, who seems as fit as a flea, may have just developed the characteristic sore throat and will be brimming with viral infection. So steering clear of virus carriers requires a little more subtlety than running away from someone constantly dabbing at his nose with a sodden hankie. Here's what to look for in people at the most infectious stage:

1) They're pale and have pinched-looking faces, with dark shadows under the eyes.
2) They may be wearing more clothing than expected. For example, an unseasonable scarf could signal a sore throat.
3) Their adam's apple may bob up and down as they swallow a lot to relieve a sore throat.
4) They don't chatter much.
5) A few sufferers have a cold sore on their lip. This may be in the form of an eruption. Towards the end of a cold, when the chances of infection have receded, it will have turned into a scab.

This kind of sleuthing should be unnecessary if you know the sufferer well – it's only good manners that family and colleagues should let you know if they're about to go under.

Avoiding Cold-givers At Home

It's difficult to keep space between yourself and a sniffler in the family home. While it would be sensible to ask your partner to sleep in a different bed for the first few nights, the suggestion may get a frosty reception. Try it anyway.

If a child succumbs, keep him or her in bed. This will hopefully confine the viruses to one bedroom, the bathroom and the toilet. If a working adult begins an itchy throat, suggest they go to office or factory as usual. Research shows conclusively, if surprisingly, that a scant number of colds are contracted at work – certainly far fewer than the home-grown variety.

Victims should have their own face cloth and towel. Don't touch it whatever you do, and give a wide berth to their sopping handkerchiefs. Viruses can live for hours in wet conditions. An ordinary piece of soap can act as a resting-place for viruses, so make sure a cold-sufferer has his own bar.

Perilous surfaces when there's a cold about also include door handles, cups, plates and cutlery, and the telephone. Always wash a cold victim's plates and cups carefully. And duck for cover when hankies are taken out with a flourish and wafted about. It's possible to buy sprays to disinfect rooms. But this would have to be done thoroughly, and many patients might find this objectionable.

Tips on Hand-washing

Sufferers and anyone near them should always wash their hands carefully and often. Here's how:
* Use soap and water, which needn't be scalding hot.
* Rub the soap into the backs and wrists – many people only wash the palms.
* Nearly everyone forgets to wash the thumbs.
* Use a brush to clean under the fingernails, an ideal hiding place for germs.
* Keep washing for at least a minute.

* If you need to wash your face, clean your hands first.
* Waving your hands about in the air is the best way to dry them. Otherwise use a clean towel or you'll recoat them with more bugs.

Masking Your Symptoms

Some parents frighten their cold-ridden children by suddenly appearing at their bedsides in white masks. These can be bought at the chemist's and worn to stop someone else's virus-laden mucus flying up your nose. But you can't guarantee to fend off a cold by this means. Viruses are tiny enough to pass through laboratory filters fine enough to trap bacteria, so there is little chance that these ordinary masks are going to intercept all the cold bugs. The same applies, of course, to those cold sufferers who considerately, if pointlessly, wear masks in the hope of keeping their infection to themselves. They rarely wear them for long anyway because the effort of inhaling through already congested tubes can make breathing very uncomfortable.

I can well remember turning up at my dentist's to find her masked-up like a surgeon at the operating table. She explained that she had a cold and didn't want to spread it. Shortly after this, and despite the mask, I had a cold too.

Of course, this could have been a coincidence, and not a very remarkable one at that. And when you remember that most airborne viruses travel on what are known in the trade as 'coarse droplets', it may be worthwhile putting masks on infected dentists, who are dealing with people face to face at close quarters. It may also be worth wearing a mask if a member of your household is undergoing any medication which could lower their natural resistance to infection.

Avoiding Colds on Public Transport

Many people who move to London from elsewhere in the UK spend much of their first two years there with streaming noses. This is because, in the Underground during the rush-hour, passengers are jammed together for minutes on end. Evasive action can be taken by turning the head, so your nearest fellow-passenger is breathing on your neck rather than into your face. If you are lucky, any cold viruses issuing from him will now pass harmlessly, avoiding your nose and eyes.

Sitting directly opposite a cold-sufferer on a bus or train is more risky than sitting by his side. Micro-organisms may fly out in a wide cone shape, like old iron from a blunderbuss, rather than a bullet from a rifle, but they still find it hard to turn corners.

The wisest course, if you are not packed in like sardines, is to move away if a nearby passenger has a cold. On a bus, move from upstairs to downstairs; on a train, change coaches.

Keeping Free of Viruses at Work

In one experiment, healthy volunteers were left in a room for different periods of time with someone who had a cold. Those staying for an hour were unaffected. Of those who remained for eight hours, only a few showed symptoms later. But nearly all those who were still there after 12 hours developed the usual problems.

Other viruses – polio, for instance – gain a hold more quickly than this. That's why doctors, who encounter multitudes of rhinoviruses, but only during short consul-tations, aren't racked with wheezes and sneezes most of the time. Similarly, if you are a salesman, or hold some other job that involves travelling and having many brief meetings with business contacts, the chances of your picking up colds from them are slight. And in the daily lives of most of us, the usual brief encounters with bank tellers, shop assistants, accountants, solicitors and so on carry only a small risk.

Of course, you may be unlucky. Unlike the lone swallow and summer, just one organism, which would show up as an isolated dot on an extra-powerful microscope, can make an infection.

People who are more vulnerable are those who congregate

in groups at work – teachers, child-minders, musicians, actors, armed services personnel and factory workers. At the opposite extreme are those who tend to be untroubled by colds because they work outdoors, where the bugs are soon dispersed. Gardeners, farm workers, builders, traffic wardens and surveyors are in this group.

How to Avoid a Christmas Cold

Christmas and New Year are the second most popular period for catching colds (the prime time is October). It's also the time of the year when our taste buds, sense of smell, voice and social spirit, should all be in tip-top condition. A cold puts paid to them all.

How many of your Yuletide family parties have been dampened because half the guests were blocked up, streaming and grumpy? How many Christmas puddings have you failed to savour – and not just because you're stuffed to bursting with turkey?

Take heart. It's possible to cut the risks of a Christmas cold by 60 per cent – but only if you are prepared to follow a highly disciplined regime in the weeks leading up to the holiday period. In fact it's worth serious consideration only if you really enjoy a family Christmas and can't stand the thought of yet another seasonal stinker.

The plan is based on avoiding crowds and stress during the holiday run-up.

* Do all your present buying well in advance. The July sales is a good time. Many presents can also be bought by mail order.
* Write your cards before December and keep them ready for instant posting.
* Do any last-minute shopping in open-air markets.
* Avoid public transport after 13 December.
* Take part of your annual holiday just before Christmas, then you won't run a gauntlet of microbes from colleagues.
* Try not to lose sleep and become run down by staying late at pre-Christmas parties. Circulate away from guests with damp hankies and bright red noses.

Slow Down and Beat the Cold

Many of the amazing advances in technology over the past 20 years or so are supposed to make life easier for everyone. What a hope! In fact, the pace of general existence is increasing relentlessly because of the 'improvements', and we have to dash around ever faster merely to keep up. All this extra effort against the clock causes worry, tension and stress – and this, as we have seen, makes us easy pickings for the cold virus.

How to slow down? Well, here are a few pointers. In total, they read like a prescription for sainthood. But there's no doubt that if you can make a start on at least some of them you will improve your chance of avoiding the usual dreary round of colds.

At Work

* Stop competing with rivals. Don't stab them in the back. People who strive for promotion aren't always as successful as those who don't. Don't waste emotional energy bearing grudges. Try to like colleagues. Look for their better points.
* Delegate as much as you can. It's easy if you don't expect others to achieve your own standards. Refuse to get upset if they don't.
* Cut down on commuting by moving nearer to your office or factory. Walk to work and back. Take the slower route if it's prettier – through a park, for instance.
* Leave for home earlier. Try to avoid taking work home. If your work-load gets unreasonable, don't suffer in silence; tell the boss.
* If you have a business appointment, set off early to avoid fretting if you are delayed.
* Cut down on your coffee and tea intake with its stimulating caffeine. Avoid junk food.
* Take up all your holiday entitlement.
* Stop striving for perfection. You'll never achieve it – and

Cut down on commuting by moving nearer to your office

everyone would hate you if you did!

At Play

* Start a relaxing hobby like gardening.
* Give up over-strenuous exercise which could divert energy from your immune system. Eschew competitive sports if they cause you stress.
* Spend more time outdoors. Foster an interest in nature. Learn to recognize different species of birds and plants. Don't wait for fine weather to go out – let the rain splash on your face.
* Play more with your children.
* Take more holidays at home, rather than undertaking the onerous preparations for a holiday abroad. If you do go to a sunnier clime, don't feel guilty about lolling on the beach.

At Home

* Talk less and listen more.
* Sleep a lot. Build up your unconscious hours by going to bed earlier by another 10 minutes every night for a week.
* Share your troubles with someone else.
* Get rid of junk in the home. Ask yourself whether you'll need any item again in the next 12 months. If the answer's no, dispose of it. There's no need, for example, to keep most paperbacks once you've read them.

Winning the Cold War

All suggestions in this chapter are based on carefully controlled scientific research into the prevention and cure of colds. If you follow all the advice, or even some of it, it would be surprising if you didn't experience fewer and much briefer coughing and sneezing bouts in the future.

It may take a little time to equip your body to fight the daily onslaught of hostile viruses. But eventually you may even build up the biological defences to banish colds for ever.

Over-the-Counter Treatments

Where would high street pharmacies be without the common cold? Britons spend £172 million a year on pills, powders, potions, sprays, syrups, vapour rubs and lozenges. £21 million goes on throat sweets alone. In the United States, which shares the dubious distinction with Britain of having more colds than anywhere else, two billion dollars a year is spent on medicines. One store in Washington DC was found to stock 38 different cough syrups and 22 kinds of nasal spray.

Come the snuffly season of October, every commercial break on television includes at least one advert for a cold reliever (you can hardly call them cures), and the hard-selling campaigns bang on through the winter. It's interesting that most of the humorous little films used to sell these products feature men bumbling around in a state of red-nosed misery. Male hypochondria is the key to bigger sales. Studies show that men can't tolerate cold symptoms as well as women.

TV campaigns seem to work. Among throat soothers, Tunes, one of the most heavily advertised, attract sales of nearly £6 million, while other brands also enjoy a mass market. They don't claim to cure a cold, of course, but to some extent help to ease some of the symptoms. There are also a variety of more strictly medicinal products available for cold sufferers. Let's see what they are and whether they will do you any good.

What's On Offer

Viruses don't cause any discomfort until they have
penetrated a human cell. Since we are unaware of their
presence before this stage, we can't take any action early
enough to kill them. The drugs at present available to us
cannot dispatch cold viruses, but some do, to a greater or
lesser extent, relieve the symptoms. Most medicines won't
shorten the illness's duration. However, the widely held
view that taking something for a cold merely prolongs the
condition doesn't stand up to scrutiny.

There are four main types of cold remedy on sale:
antihistamines, decongestants, pain-killers and cough
medicines.

Antihistamines

As the name implies, these neutralize the effects of
histamine, a chemical produced by the body which helps to
promote allergic reactions to household dust, pollen and
many other airborne irritants. The sneezing, watery nose and
scarlet eyes of hay-fever sufferers are all caused by histamine.
Benefit: Antihistamines are extremely useful against allergies, and they are believed to help dry up the similar
symptoms of a cold, though some experts are sceptical.
Disadvantages: Some antihistamine preparations make you
drowsy.

Decongestants

During a cold, and especially in its later stages, blood cells
swell up inside the nose. Together with the increased flow of
discharge, this blocks the passages. A decongestant taken by
a pocket spray reduces the blood cells to normal size. You
can also buy decongestants in tablet form.
Benefits: This is one of those rare medicines which has an
almost immediate effect. One spray up each nostril clears a
very congested nose for up to eight hours. This is especially

useful in helping you get a full night's sleep. Sprays also prevent a build-up of mucus, which could lead to sinusitis.

Some people say breathing steam from a bowl of hot water with eucalyptus in it has the same effect. True – but it's less convenient, nor is the effect as long-lasting. Of the sprays available, you may prefer brands that do not contain aromatics.

Disadvantages: If you use nasal sprays for more than a week you may suffer something called 'rebound congestion' – which means your nose becomes stuffed up even worse than before. Your natural inclination will be to give it another squirt of spray. Don't – or the whole cycle will begin again. Moreover, your blockage may continue long after the cold's gone.

I once interviewed an office clerk who had been unable to breathe properly for months after overdoing a nasal spray. She was eventually weaned off by a doctor, who has since campaigned for the existing warnings against over-use to be stated on the spray bottle as well as on its box. Some years ago I suffered the problem after reading on a nasal spray that rebound congestion was not a problem. The manufacturers later removed this wording.

In addition, some sprays can cause a stinging sensation in the nostrils of a few people who are especially sensitive to them.

Some doctors recommend putting a salt and tap water solution into the nose with a dropper. This has no side effects, and is specially suited to children.

Overnight Chest Rubs

These usually contain ingredients with a nice old-fashioned 'wintry' smell, such as eucalyptus or camphor.

Advantages: They work gently and they smell nice. You're not likely to suffer any side effects even if you overdo it. 'Junior' versions are available for very young children who can't breathe properly at night.

Disadvantages: I find them less effective than sprays. And

people can smell that you have a cold.

Pain-killers

The aches and pains of a cold can be treated with aspirin and paracetamol. Throbbing heads, painful muscles and joints and sore throats are also relieved. Both lower the temperature if there's a fever.

Benefits: If you buy plain aspirin or paracetamol, they are inexpensive; slightly more expensive forms are soluble in water. There's little point in buying the heavily advertised proprietary brands whose only active ingredient is either aspirin or paracetamol but which are more elaborately packaged and far more expensive.

Disadvantages: Aspirin may cause stomach problems.

Cough Medicines

These are either expectorants or suppressants. The former thins the mucus, making it easier to cough up. Suppressants kill the desire to cough, which is not necessarily a good thing even though it may help you to sleep at night.

Advantages: A suppressant is best for a constant, dry, unproductive cough.

Disadvantages: Some doctors say drinking water, or warm liquids like soup, is just as effective as commercial expectorants, since they do the same job of diluting the mucus in the throat.

General Advice

By all means try any of these preparations. None of them 'cures' colds or even shortens their duration, but some may reduce the severity of some of the symptoms. As long as you read the warnings about any possible side effects, you've nothing to lose but their cost. And, as a general rule, *never* exceed the stated dose.

Colds That Changed History

The chances are high that some of our great historical figures had colds when they were making up their minds about world events.

So on the eve of battles, there may have been many a poor combatant with a dry throat and streaming eyes suffering silently lest the former was taken as a sign of terror and the latter as an example of cowardly blubbering. Nor would generals ever admit to having a cold for fear that a runny nose would detract from the glory of the moment. Hence documented cases of colds interfering with history are not common.

We may never know for certain, but in at least one military catastrophe – the Battle of Borodino – the involvement of a cold was clear.

But before we continue, we should perhaps point out that most of the colds described in this chapter occurred at a time when everyone thought getting chilly and wet caused the condition. And this, as will be demonstrated later in the theory of 'sleeping viruses', has not been entirely disproved to this day.

Napoleon – the Cold's Part in his Downfall

One of the biggest upsets in history was caused by a valet. He forgot to bring Napoleon Bonaparte his waterproof boots on 24 August 1812. As a result, Napoleon came down with one of the worst colds of his life. He had a fever, a blocked

nose, a sore throat and hoarse voice all at the same time. Which was unfortunate for him because he was in the middle of his Russian campaign and but a few days away from the decisive confrontation at Borodino. During this horrendous battle, the Emperor was slouched on a camp stool. He seemed too ill to care what was going on and the failure to send in his crack Old Guard at a crucial moment was attributed to his snuffly condition.

Although the French won, they didn't rout the Russians, so it was counted as a failure. It wasn't long after that that the discouraged emperor decided on the long march back to France, in which a large part of his army lost their lives in the Russian snow. After his Russian defeat, a demoralized Napoleon went into decline. So it is possible that a cold saved not only Russia from French domination but perhaps even Britain as well...

The Bard Catches It

The world lost its greatest writer because of a cold. William Shakespeare was 52 when he made his will in February 1616. The next month, two of his fellow poets, Michael Drayton and Ben Jonson, called on him at his home in Stratford-upon-Avon.

It is said the trio had a 'merry meeting' which does suggest an Elizabethan pub crawl. It's not known what they got up to but maybe the Bard of Avon actually fell into the Avon? Anyway, he caught a cold, which must have turned into pneumonia, because he died in his bed on his birthday a few weeks later.

Cold Bacon

The chap most often mentioned as the real writer of Shakespeare's plays also perished after a cold, although Sir Francis Bacon's illness later proved an actual boon to the modern world.

In 1626, the famous scientist and philosopher was lording it in his coach in Highgate when, gazing at the falling snow, suddenly the idea of refrigeration came upon him. He presented himself at a poor woman's cottage, bought a hen and asked her to cook it. Then he went outside and stuffed his purchase with snow. He hoped to prove that this would keep the meat as well as salt, which was the only practical food preservative at the time.

All this messing about in the freezing wet apparently gave Sir Francis a streamer. He was taken to the Earl of Arundel's home to recuperate. But the bed was damp and complications set in. However, as Sir Francis did take his hen with him to the Earl's place to keep an eye on his experiment's progress, in the three days it took him to die he realized he'd discovered – the world's first frozen chicken.

Elizabeth I

Vanity, and regret at having to deal harshly with the Earl of Essex, probably killed the Virgin Queen.

She was persuaded by her advisers that Essex was a treacherous plotter, so she was forced to do something which upset her – she ordered his head to be cut off.

Not long afterwards, in January 1603, the Queen and her court moved to Richmond and encountered some of the rawest winds ever experienced in Tudor Britain. Yet Her Majesty kept on wearing summer gowns because she thought they made her more glamorous. She had never accepted her advancing years which were nearly twice as many as those of Essex. In Richmond she caught a cold but, despite being pressed by anxious courtiers, she refused to see her doctors. It was said she was too depressed about Essex, whose ring she still wore, to want to live longer. The cold worsened, her temperature shot up and, at the age of 69, she passed away.

Before her death, Elizabeth is supposed to have called out the name of her successor, James I. There's grave doubt about this, however, as, at the time, she'd lost her voice.

Where's Me Shirt?

When Charles I lost his head over the English Civil War, he left a question unanswered. Was the royal head cold-ridden when it was laid on the block? Let's examine the evidence.

The King was, of course, under enough stress to attract a cold and he was a pessimist by nature. He also acted with great calmness as he met his death. Or was he just feeling too rotten to care? But the final piece of evidence is more convincing. As the King walked to his demise in Whitehall, he was wearing an extra undershirt. He explained that he did not want to give the impression of being afraid by shivering. And people are prone to shivering fits at the beginning of a cold...

He Died Writing

When he was 25, Germany's answer to Shakespeare wrote *Werther*, a novel so sad that people began committing suicide in sympathy. He was Johann Wolfgang von Goethe, poet, dramatist and scientist, and the world was eventually denied his genius by the common cold.

One draughty March day in 1832, the great man caught a chill while riding in his carriage. The next entry in his diary, which proved to be the last, was: 'Spent all day in bed because of indisposition.'

Four days later, a physician was sent for, who later described how the poet kept moving from his bed to a divan in a restless fury. He died shortly afterwards.

Remember the Alamo?

In 1836, Texas was fighting for independence from the Mexican dictator, Santa Anna, who fancied himself as another Napoleon. On his white horse, loaded down with medals, and in front of 4,000 men, he marched towards Texas.

In his way was a former Christian mission, called the

Alamo, manned by 183 brave souls whom General Santa Anna had decided to teach a lesson. There followed the most famous siege in American history.

The man in charge of the American forces was the inventor of the Bowie knife and a useful man to have around in a battle. Unfortunately for Texas, however, 40-year-old Jim Bowie was indisposed. His Mexican wife and children had all died after a recent smallpox outbreak. Stressed and worn out, and cooped up with so many different cold bugs from adventurers from all over America, he caught a feverish cold.

Jim Bowie is said to have put in an appearance in the open air just once. Everyone wishing to stay to face the enemy was invited to walk across a line drawn with a sabre in the dust. Bowie asked to be carried across.

When the Mexicans overran the mission they found him back in bed. He was barely able to fire a few pistols and flash his famous blade before being bayoneted to death.

So, next time you're in bed with a corker, remember that there was once a sufferer in old Texas who had a much worse deal: it's bad enough contending with a sore throat and a cough, without having to fend off thousands of screaming Mexicans who are baying for your blood.

The Alamo affair has often been filmed. But Hollywood pretends colds don't exist: Bowie is usually seen being carried to his sick bed with shrapnel wounds.

Why Queen Victoria's Dad Wasn't Amused

There would never have been a golden Victorian age without the common cold.

It happened like this: Victoria's father, the Duke of Kent, showed no desire to follow his daughter's strict morals. In fact, he fell into such debt that he was obliged to sell his own home.

Once a fortune teller told him that two members of his family would kick the royal bucket. His mentally ill father George IV or maybe his brother, the Prince Regent, he speculated.

Then the Duke went for a stroll in wintry conditions and in leaky shoes. He didn't change his sopping stockings on return and, you've guessed the rest, he caught a cold that led to a lung infection.

Some of his last words were, 'My brothers are not as strong as I am. I shall outlive them all. The crown will come to me and my children.'

Less than a week after his death, the fortune teller's second prophecy came true as George III followed suit.

The Duke's early end cost him his ambition for a son to inherit the throne. And eventually, two short reigns later, his daughter Victoria got the job.

And How George V Became King

In 1892, another lung complaint, following a cold, was again to strike Queen Victoria's family. The victim this time was her grandson Albert, Edward VII's son and heir to the throne.

As a result, Prince George Frederick Ernest Albert became Prince of Wales in 1901. Ten years later, at the age of 44 he became George V. So without Edward's cold, Queen Elizabeth wouldn't be our Queen now…

President for Four Weeks

Warring redskins never caught up with galloping frontiersman William Harrison, but a cold did. He was president of the United States for the shortest time ever – just a few weeks.

Harrison was a noted fighter for the army, coming to prominence in the Battle of Fallen Timbers against a confederation of several Indian tribes. On the strength of this he became Governor of Indiana.

Not happy about losing much of their territory to the government the Indians rebelled but, in the comically named Battle of Tippecanoe, the whites, under Harrison's experienced command, won hands down. His next venture – a campaign for the presidency – made a lot of this victory. Supporters handed out model log cabins and jugs of cider to emphasize the governor's colourful career.

It worked and Harrison was elected. However, at the inauguration ceremony, he promoted his tough-guy image by not wearing his hat and coat in the drizzle and freezing wind. He caught a cold which turned to pneumonia and he perished on 4 March 1841.

And then, no doubt, a few impoverished Indians did a war dance on the grave of North America's briefest president.

Colds and Vitamin C

Taking ascorbic acid or, as it's better known, vitamin C is easily the most popular self-treatment for a common cold. There really is a remarkable amount of faith in it: people who deride all other cures will often say 'I don't believe in treating a cold. I only take Vitamin C'.

Ascorbic acid is found in citrus fruits – orange, lemon, grapefruit, etc – and in leafy green vegetables. One doctor I spoke to in West Yorkshire ate 10 oranges a day and claimed to have been a stranger to colds since starting her juicy regime. That is no mean feat for a GP who encounters scores of infected throats every week. It's also good news for orange farmers.

Yet half the medical profession is equally convinced that the vitamin is of no use whatsoever against cold infection.

The belief in vitamin C as a cold cure has been with us some time. One scientific study on the subject was published in Australia in 1947, and others have been carried out at frequent intervals since.

Before they closed shop in 1991, scientists at the Cold Research Centre in Salisbury, Wiltshire, were telling every journalist who asked that vitamin C's contribution to the cold war was nil. But an American Nobel Prize winner for Chemistry, Professor Linus Pauling, gathered evidence to the contrary. His argument, published in 1970, was that scientists who had 'proved' that vitamin C was useless had not dosed their volunteers with the large amounts needed to make a difference.

Since he first voiced his support, many studies have been made by eminent researchers using various amounts of ascorbic acid. And though the results have been patchy, most have shown that taking extra vitamin C will reduce the duration and symptoms to some extent.

Unfortunately, evidence to support the view that taking vitamin C will cut down the number of colds you get is scanty. 'No study has ever shown it to be an effective cold preventative', asserts a report published by the University of California. However, the validity of that pronouncement depends on your definition of 'effective'. There is probably enough scientific evidence around to convince reasonable people that taking vitamin C to prevent colds is at least worth a try, and that stepping up the dosage when a cold is under way is an even better bet.

What is Vitamin C?

Ascorbic acid was discovered by a Hungarian chemist, Albert S. Zent-Gyorgyi, as recently as 1932. Which is rather odd because, as anyone who reads pirate stories will know, a shortage of the stuff consigned thousands of old-time sailors to death from scurvy.

A sailor on Captain James Cook's ship *Resolution* in 1773 wrote this song:

> We were all hearty seamen, no colds did we
>   fear,
> And we have from all sickness entirely kept
>   clear,
> Thanks be to the captain, he has proved so
>   good,
> Amongst all the islands to give us fresh food.

Captain Cook was a stickler for healthy eating on his long voyages, making his crew eat fresh green vegetables and the juice of lemons. He was the first naval explorer to demonstrate the effectiveness of a good diet in combating scurvy, which until his time had accounted for far more deaths at sea than all the naval battles of history.

How Vitamin C May Cure Colds

Ascorbic acid is known to chemists as an antioxidant: this means it is hostile to oxygen and will destroy it. When cold viruses attach themselves to a human cell, the cell releases oxygen-bearing compounds which inflame tissues in the nose, causing the classic symptoms.

The inflammatory compounds are substances called oxidants, and ascorbic acid breaks them down. So the swelling dies down, and so do the cold symptoms.

That, at any rate, is the theory. Some laboratory analysis suggests that colds treated with high doses of vitamin C are suppressed rather than terminated. In other words, if you don't keep on taking the pills for some days after the symptoms disappear, they'll soon come back.

Can You Take Too Much Vitamin C?

Until recently, even extremely large doses of vitamin C were thought to be free of side effects (which is not true of some other vitamins). Many experts are still convinced that taking a lot of vitamin C is harmless, apart from causing you to go to the lavatory more than usual. But some researchers in the United States assert that very large doses could cause nausea, abdominal cramps, diarrhoea and kidney stones.

There's some evidence that taking hefty doses of vitamin C could actually give you more colds in your lifetime. But this shouldn't stop you taking it. An American study, carried out over 10 years, suggested that men consuming artificial vitamin C lived six years longer than those who did not. That's time to have another 18 infections – if the pills don't also work to prevent them.

The Verdict

For what it's worth, I once took vitamin C for a year, during which time I had only one short cold. However, I took large doses which cost a lot. The next year I continued faithfully with this regime – and caught one cold after another!

Researchers who support vitamin C claim that every published research project so far has shown some statistics in favour of the chemical. Sometimes it hasn't made much difference to patients, but it has always made *some* difference. These researchers took precautions to rule out the placebo effect. So people who take vitamin C may have the added advantage of believing in it – which could, as with all remedies, make it more effective.

So if you think it works for you, then go ahead. But remember you'll need to take between one and two grams a day. And stagger the regime.

Where to Find It

If you hope to prevent or cure colds you'll need to take much more of it than is available in fruits and vegetables. So you will have to resort to pharmaceutical ascorbic acid. But don't worry – it's exactly the same as natural vitamin C.

Chemists' shops sell it in the form of pills or as fizzy tablets which dissolve in water to make an orange-flavoured drink. But the cheapest way is to buy it in crystal form in large quantities. Sometimes you'll need to order it in advance.

Colds and Zinc

The story goes that a little American boy was in hospital. He had an illness made worse by a deficiency of the metal zinc. He also had a cold. He was given hefty doses of zinc. What happened to his other complaint isn't reported, but the cold dried up as quick as lightning. Following a wave of publicity, enterprising companies began selling zinc tablets to relieve cold symptoms.

But does it work?

What the Boffins Say

A company set up to market zinc in the United States pointed triumphantly to one scientific study which showed that, with zinc tablets, the length of colds was cut by two-fifths. This study was based on trials carried out by the Dartmouth College Health Service in Hanover, New Hampshire.

You have to be very careful with experiments into possible medical cures. And this test fulfilled all the best criteria by being a 'randomized, placebo-controlled, double-blind trial'. As many research projects into viral behaviour are carried out on these strict lines, it's worth explaining the jargon.

'Randomized' means the volunteers are picked at random from, say, a list of those eligible to vote in a particular region. They're not singled out, for example, for their age, or sex or known susceptibility to infection.

The second condition calls for the use of placebos. These are dummy pills which look exactly like the pills under test.

'Placebo-controlled' means that half the volunteers take pills containing the active substance, and the others are given these fake tablets. None of the volunteers knows which pills he or she is using.

Such a test would be 'blind' because, to be on the safe side, the volunteers do not even know placebos are being used. Now because the researchers might give this fact away, by their body language if nothing else, the more stringent experiments are 'double blind', which means even the test organizers don't know which volunteers get dummy pills and which take the real thing. This information is held by a third party.

The Dartford Experiment

The 70 young people who took part in the trials at Dartford each kept a diary of their cold symptoms. These disappeared in a little less than five full days for the volunteers dosed with zinc, while those who took the placebo pills suffered for just over six days.

There was a more dramatic result for cold-sufferers who were given zinc a full day after the signs of a cold began to appear. The colds lasted another four days in zinc-taking patients, compared to an extra nine days for patients taking the fake pills.

The experimenters found that zinc was particularly effective in relieving blocked noses and coughs.

How Does Zinc Work?

Two theories have been put forward:
1) Some viruses don't do at all well in environments rich in zinc.
2) Thymulin, a hormone which helps to develop T cells, needs zinc. T cells are carried by white blood cells to the scene of infections to do battle with viruses.

As we've seen, colds impair our performance in all sorts of ways. For example, a motorist is five times more dangerous with a heavy cold than he would be if he was driving with just under the alcohol limit. But research trials have shown that zinc improves our concentration during a cold.

Taking Zinc

If you decide to take zinc supplements, it's important to know that exceeding the recommended dose may reduce the body's ability to absorb another essential metal, copper. Never take more than 20 mg of zinc per day. One way of telling you if you have a copper deficiency is to examine your finger nails for white flecks.

In general, it looks as though zinc can alleviate the effects of a cold, especially if it's taken as soon as the symptoms appear.

The Social Niceties

An unhappy consequence of going under with a real streamer is that personal goals tend to take a back seat. It's not just a result of feeling unwell; it seems to be a genuine symptom of a cold that you just don't care about things as you normally would. Your desire to go out and seek an attractive mate is diluted. Your career ambitions go on the back burner. And as for those carefully laid plans for redecorating the spare room – do me a favour!

Sufferers tend to use their answer machines because they can't be bothered with telephone conversations. They neglect their appearance and slope off early from social occasions. But as no one is ever forgiven for letting their standards slither, even in illness, the cold victim must make an effort. He or she must work harder still to overcome the more unattractive aspects of their temporary condition.

How to Appear in Public

Thankfully, even the worst colds don't have the same disfiguring visual effects as some other common illnesses like mumps, measles or chicken-pox. But an angry red nose with twin dribbles heading southwards certainly lacks charm, while a mouth hanging open because it's the only available channel through which to draw breath is a little short on charisma.

So here are a few tips for improving your appearance.
* Use best-quality cotton handkerchiefs. A finely-woven

cloth is less likely to abrade your nostrils.
* Don't blow your nose too often in the early stages. A lot of mucus will drip harmlessly down your gullet. But when the discharge begins to thicken you'll need to do a bit more blowing; otherwise it may collect in your sinuses and cause painful inflammation.
* Dab away any moisture between the nose end and the upper lip, otherwise the skin will chap.
* The great outdoors, especially if there's an ill wind, will make an angry nose look worse. Try to stay inside.
* Use a lip salve to smear a thin protective layer just below the nostrils. Don't overdo it, otherwise it will look like a permanent drip.
* Don't pull at your face or massage your eyes to relieve painful sinuses. It won't do any good and will make you look haggard.
* Speak softly to preserve your voice.
* It's not always as obvious to a cold sufferer as it is to other people that a couple of 'dew drops' have quietly appeared at the nose end. Keep checking.

The Cold Code

When we develop a cold there are effects on other people, so try to observe the following code of manners.
* Tell people that you have a cold, so they can avoid you if they choose to.
* Don't call at someone's home with a cold unless you've warned them first. They may worry about catching it, and there may also be a patient in the house who must avoid all infections.
* Blow your nose quietly. Resist the temptation to peer into your handkerchief like someone reading the tea-leaves at the bottom of a cup.
* Use a nasal spray only when nobody's looking.
  Don't be a constant sniffer, especially on public transport.
* No prizes are awarded for the noisiest sneeze of the year.
* Don't waft your germ-laden hankie about or leave it lying

Tell people you have a cold

around. A scientific examination of a handkerchief after 30 seconds' use was found to contain 15,000 germs.
* A green hankie is better than a white one – for unpleasantly obvious reasons.
* If you have a lengthy coughing fit at night, and you share your bedroom with someone, go downstairs out of earshot for a cup of tea. There's no point in two people going without sleep.
* Suffer silently. Don't whinge!

How to Be a Cold Bore

A quick way to lose friends, enrage colleagues and alienate the family.
* If someone asks 'How are you?', back them into a corner and give them a full account of all your symptoms.
* Take handfuls of other people's paper tissues.
* Blow your nose with gusto, and wake the dead with your coughs and sneezes.
* Use only one handkerchief.
* Over-imbibe at parties. There are few nastier sights than a drunk with a streaming cold.
* Call out your GP on a rain-drenched winter night.

How to Pamper Yourself

* Go to bed with a comforting hot-water bottle. Better still, take two.
* Treat yourself to your favourite tit-bits, even junk food if you must.
* Spend several evenings by a real fire with a good book. Disconnect the phone.
* Drink whisky with honey and a generous squeeze of lemon in a glass of hot water. It won't cure your cold, but if you have enough of it you won't care!
* Smear your upper chest with a vapour rub at night.

Mind Over Matter

Colds come in various grades of severity, from fleeting sniffles to real corkers. But you'll notice that some people remain cheerfully normal whatever the severity of their symptoms, while others seem to suffer a mental as well as physical collapse even with the mildest attack. Even allowing for tight-lipped fanatics on the one side and natural whingers on the other, it's clear that colds really do affect different people in different ways.

Nonetheless, the question still arises as to the best way to respond to a cold. Do we compel ourselves to use up the normal amount of energy getting our work done, following our hobbies and fulfilling social engagements? Or should we cancel everything, have a few days in bed, and devote ourselves to some serious self-pampering?

Before deciding whether to be a 'cold-ignorer' or a 'cold-acceptor', consider whether it's actually possible to put a cold to the back of your mind. One Christmas I tried to convince myself I hadn't got a cold when my throat was painful, my nose was dripping, and my head thumped. I took no medicine or vitamin C, put on no extra clothing, drank no extra fluids, did a lot of strenuous partying and went to bed late.

After three days of this, I suddenly felt ghastly, my nose was totally blocked, my throat felt like someone had gone over it with sandpaper, and my temples throbbed like a road-pounder. That year I saw in the New Year from my bed. I'm convinced that the cold, having been earlier ignored, wreaked revenge by gathering strength and lasting longer.

Colds at Work

This failure to master a cold by will-power happened in a holiday atmosphere, when people are relaxed. It's easier to ignore the symptoms if you have serious tasks in hand – if you're a barrister making your final speech for the defence, say, or a sapper clearing a minefield. The symptoms don't disappear just because there is vital work to be done, but you'll feel them less if you make a deliberate effort not to think about them.

This trick can be worked only because cold symptoms are at worst irritating. They don't cause searing pain, or threaten to cost you a limb or an organ. True, a cold makes you feel lousy, but the feeling is generalized and comes and goes, so the mind can control its response to it.

Another way of manipulating colds is to concentrate on some other complaint, like a backache or an ankle strain. The brain tends to cope with only one medical problem at a time. So while you're thinking about a painful condition, your cold is on the back burner for an hour or two. You won't benefit from this course of action, of course, unless you happen to prefer back pain or whatever to your cold miseries.

The News Effect

This is a common experience, which shows that the mind *can* put a cold in its place, if only temporarily. The worst case of sniffles you've ever had is building to a climax. You feel terrible. Then the phone rings. You hear you've been promoted. You put the receiver down quietly enough, but then jump up and down with joy. All the symptoms have suddenly vanished. This relief sometimes lasts for several hours before the malaise starts to reassert itself.

Curiously enough, receiving bad news has exactly the same effect. If your accountant phones to say you've gone bankrupt, your cold will also be forgotten – temporarily.

Colds and Children

'Oh daughter dear,' her mother said, 'this
  blanket around you fold,
'Tis such a dreadful night abroad, you will catch
  your death of cold.'
  – From *Young Charlotte*,
  by William Lorenzo Carter (1813–60)

Babies

Cold viruses waste no time in attacking humans. It isn't long
before they welcome your progeny into the world with a
dose of the sniffles. This early introduction is no surprise
since babies have had little time to build up their immune
systems. Any virus-carrier who leans over them in adoration,
whether they are suffering symptoms or not, may trigger the
first illness of a baby's life.

Often, of course, this is its mother who may be overrun
with cold viruses on giving birth. The mental and physical
stress of impending childbirth will weaken a woman's
immunity to infection, turning her nose and throat into a
viral playground.

Babies who are breast-fed do get some instant immunity
from colds from their mother's milk. (The benefits of this
inheritance seem to decrease after about six months, at which
time colds come on with a vengeance.) Mother's milk has
been found to contain a substance rich in the white cells that
are also present in the blood and which, as we've seen, put a

strait-jacket on viruses. These white cells in the milk are more effective against cold bugs than the white cells in the baby's blood because they go straight to the site of the infection. Baby has the handy means to suck an anti-viral agent straight into its throat.

Experimental research in Britain and Sweden in the 1950s showed that babies on bottle milk had more colds (and other illnesses) than those who were breast-fed.

Why Babies Struggle with Colds

Small babies have a tough time with a cold. The extra flow of mucus quickly blocks their tiny airways. It is very hard to breathe through the mouth while sucking on the breast or bottle. So it's best to see your doctor if your baby catches cold in its first three months.

Blockades can be cleared from a baby's nostrils with a mixture of salt and water. Parents should ask a nurse or midwife to show them how it's done. Basically, the technique involves laying the child on its back across the lap. The head is supported but allowed to drop back slightly. One or two drops of the mixture are popped into each nostril with a dropper. After 30 seconds with the head held still, the baby is seated upright with its head slightly forward. It should be able to breathe more freely and feed normally.

Babies as Cold Spreaders

Although they can't, alas, blow their noses, babies are able to cough and sneeze in a most adult fashion. And without the use of a hankie to intercept the bugs, they are adept at distributing colds around the family.

How to Stop Your Baby Getting Colds

If you ask a health visitor how to protect your baby from your streamer, she may say 'Try not to breathe over her'. If there is any advantage at all to this dubious advice it's that it enables

either mum or dad to hand the sole responsibility for
changing nappies to the fit partner for a while.

Another daft course is to keep your baby away from other
infants in case she catches something. In fact, the sooner she
does develop the customary string of colds, the quicker her
antibodies will build up and the quicker the severity of the
symptoms will be reduced. (Though, for reasons given
earlier, it's wise to protect very young babies from visiting
cold bearers.)

Toddlers and Colds

Once a toddler starts mixing with others in nurseries and
play groups, the viruses will get started in earnest, and his or
her nose may appear to be running all the time.

Children attract more colds than adults because their
standards of hygiene are pretty low. Toddlers like picking
their noses, using fingers which have touched other sticky
hands which have probably just done the same thing. This is
the perfect way for a cold virus to travel: it doesn't even have
to undertake a perilous journey by air. Young children
should be taught to blow their noses as early as possible, and
then often. If mucus builds up it becomes easier for
secondary infections to set in, including asthma and
infections of the middle ear – and even (though much more
rarely) pneumonia and meningitis.

Don't feel too worried, however, when your children catch
ordinary colds. Psychologists say they are much more
tolerant of the symptoms. That's why you'll often see a
two-year-old smile after a fit of coughing. As they get older
they tend to become more grumpy with a cold, but don't
expect one to slow them down.

Treating Younger Children

High street chemists make lots of money selling a wide range
of symptom-relievers for children – from junior analgesics to
deal with pain and fever to a welter of cough medicines. Read

the labels on all these products very carefully. Make sure any medicine you buy is for your child's age group, and that you get the dosage exactly right. Small bodies aren't as resilient to overdoses as adult ones. Make a point of asking the pharmacist – that is, the one with the qualifications – for his advice rather than choosing a product on the basis of a friend's advice or an ad. in the papers.

There's a lot you can do for your children without buying drugs. Studies have shown that symptoms among children will worsen if they are exposed to chilly fresh air. So keep them in a uniformly warm room for a few days. Bed is the best place, if only because this may confine the viruses to one room of the house.

Many youngsters smitten by colds lose their appetite. You may have to resort to their favourite foods for a bit, even if they're not as nourishing as their regular diet. But even if they refuse all solid food for a day or two, there's no need to worry, as long as they get plenty to drink.

Toddlers respond to tender loving care, but do not overdo the sympathy. The main thing is to give them frequent assurance that the sore throat, blocked nose, cough and other misery-making symptoms will soon be over.

A good way to deflect a toddler's attention away from her woes is to tell her that his or her favourite cuddly doll has also come down with the cold. Tuck the doll into bed with your child, telling them that the doll needs nursing too.

Cold Complications in Children

Many of the diseases which bedevil childhood begin with the same symptoms as those of a cold, including chicken-pox, measles, whooping cough and scarlet fever.

Obviously you shouldn't call the doctor every time your child gets a dry throat. But you should certainly ask him to call if your child begins what appears to be a cold with a very severe sore throat or a high temperature. These are good indications that something more serious is taking hold. The average normal body temperature for children (and adults) is

37°C or 98.6°F, and even a nasty cold rarely raises the temperature by more than one or two degrees Fahrenheit.

Tonsillitis

When a child gets a cold he nearly always suffers mild tonsillitis. The tonsils are two wads of tissue on either side of the back of the throat. They are part of the lymph system and their function is to filter out cold viruses and other micro-nuisances which have entered through the nose and mouth and to prevent them travelling downwards to cause problems in the lungs.

Until a few decades ago it was common for children to have their tonsils removed because the medical profession believed – quite wrongly – that they caused colds. It has now been proved beyond doubt that children who have had their tonsils removed catch as many colds as those who have not. So this operation is never carried out nowadays merely as an anti-cold measure.

During a severe attack of tonsillitis, the young victim feels really off colour. He has a temperature, glands in his neck swell, and – surprisingly – his stomach tissues become inflamed and cause tummy ache.

If cold viruses are to blame your doctor can't do much about it, and the complaint must run its course. But you should certainly consult the doctor as he may well wish to prescribe antibiotics in case bacteria have also been taking hold. In general, however, the tonsils are equipped to handle marauding germs and the illness usually clears up in a few days. Meanwhile, you can give a child over twelve aspirin – but first of all, read the instructions on the label carefully. He or she should also drink plenty of water and fruit juice.

Earache

This common complication of a cold develops when the infection migrates from the throat to the inner ear. The resultant inflammation, known as otitis media, is what causes the ear to ache. Your GP should be called within 12 hours. A hot-water bottle held to the ear may ease the pain until he arrives. A course of antibiotics puts matters right.

Whooping Cough

This is a nasty affliction which often begins like a cold, though it's caused by bacteria rather than viruses. In mild cases the symptoms are a runny nose, an unspectacular fever and a bit of a cough. But the cough often gets worse, coming in spasms. It's followed by a characteristic whooping sound. There may also be vomiting as a thick mucus is brought up. This will go on for six to eight weeks. In the worst cases, whooping cough can cause brain damage and it can even be fatal.

Call the doctor at the very first signs. He may decide that the child should go into hospital for treatment. Nowadays, immunization has considerably reduced the threat of what once was a dangerous scourge in children.

Pneumonia

The danger of this disease, once a killer of millions, has been very much curtailed by antibiotics. It often begins as a complication of a cold. Call a doctor if your child becomes drowsy or the skin turns blue, and the temperature higher than normal for a cold. The symptoms may also include a cough.

Bronchitis

This affects the windpipe and the bronchial tubes which branch off the windpipe and carry air into the lungs. During a cold, infection can spread downwards, causing inflammation. Watch out for a cold which fails to clear up as quickly as usual or which suddenly worsens.

In bronchitis there'll be a dry cough which comes not from the throat (as in a cold) but from the chest. Cough medicine may help, but consult a doctor first. The illness usually runs its course in a week to 10 days.

An old wives' tale asserts that teething causes bronchitis. It doesn't. But because the process of teething lowers a child's resistance to infection, the two problems may arise at the same time.

Bronchiolitis

It's a pity the name of this condition is so like that of bronchitis, because to confuse the two could be dangerous. Bronchiolitis is in fact another problem in the chest which can start as a cold. It's a fairly rare condition which most often affects babies between 12 months and two years of age. It requires a doctor's immediate attention, and he may arrange for the child to go into hospital.

The viruses responsible invade the bronchioles, which are tiny branches that lead off the bronchial tubes all over the lungs. They become inflamed and breathing is difficult. The patient takes rapid, shallow, wheezy breaths. There's coughing, a slight temperature and a reluctance to eat.

Children and Stress

As we've seen, one of the best weapons against the onset of colds is to reduce stress. Children suffer from this affliction just as much as adults. In fact, a child worried about a spotty face or an unfounded belief that his head is larger than normal is probably more stressed than an adult moving house.

If your offspring seems extra quiet, spend time trying to find the reason so you can put the matter right or at least take appropriate action. Children are likely to suffer stress for what parents may consider trivial reasons – if they're made to eat foods they don't like, for instance, or forced to wear clothes they feel foolish in. In these circumstances, if you insist on getting your own way it is quite possible that they will get more colds than usual and become vulnerable to other infections too.

Try These Cures!

'There's nothing you can do, you'll just have to let it run its course'. These discouraging words are all too often heard from family doctors.

Of course, there are many proprietary medicines available which cannot cure a cold, even though they are masquerading as 'cold remedies' in chemists' shops. But the idea that there's nothing you can do to avoid, shorten or ease colds is far from the truth. In this chapter I've tried to sort the sheep from the goats in cold prevention and treatment. All the advice which follows is based on research carried out in universities and other centres with a reputation for serious scientific inquiry.

Steaming

Method: Pour a kettleful of not-quite boiling water into a large bowl. Drape a small towel around your head and over the bowl. When the steam is at a bearable temperature breathe it in deeply through the nose. Keep this up for at least 15 minutes, topping up the hot water as necessary.

How it works: The steam loosens the products of catarrh. It also eases a sore throat and converts a hoarse croak into a normal voice. This age-old remedy has also been shown recently to reduce the *duration* of a cold. The *British Medical Journal* has reported careful experiments in which inhaling moist air at a temperature of 43°C (109.4°F) for half an hour cut symptoms by nearly a half. The assumption is that warm

71

steam neutralizes or inhibits viruses, which prefer a lower temperature.

Pros and Cons: Unlike some decongestant sprays (when they're used longer than recommended by the makers), breathing steam won't result in greater congestion later.

Steam-Plus

Method: As above, but with the addition of eucalyptus oil or a medicinal balsam to the water; and beef up the aroma with sage or peppermint leaves. Alternatively, add a spoonful of a proprietary vapour rub into the bowl.

How it works: The pungent vapours enhance the steam's ability to cut through the blockage.

Pros and Cons: More enjoyable than breathing in steam – but more expensive too.

Soft Drinks & Soups

Method: Drink plenty of water, fruit juices and squashes, and soups. Use hot water to dilute squash.

How it works: If you have a fever your body sweats, thus losing moisture. Drinking more helps to prevent you becoming dehydrated. Hot drinks also keep up the temperature at the site of infection (the throat and nose). As we have seen already viruses don't like too much heat.

Pros and Cons: If you're living on your own and feeling lousy, preparing drinks is obviously less trouble than cooking food. On the other hand, assuming your appetite is normal, try to eat your usual amount, possibly a little more.

The Hard Stuff

Method: Have a pint of beer, a whisky, a gin and tonic or two glasses of wine a day.

How it works: see 'The Booze Cure', page 117.

Pros and Cons: Until now, most people who've taken whisky for colds have admitted to themselves that this was not *really* for medicinal purposes. Now they can do so with a clear conscience.

Sleep

Method: A regular eight hours a night will help to prevent colds. As soon as the first signs appear, try to get 10 hours a night.

How it works: Your immune system is restored and strengthened as you rest.

Pros and Cons: If you stay in bed, you won't spread germs among friends and colleagues.

Decongestant Sprays

Method: One squirt up each nostril while breathing in fiercely.

How they work: see 'Over-the-Counter Treatments', page 39.

Pros and Cons: Very effective when the nose is completely blocked towards the end of a cold. One dose lasts up to eight hours. But if you over-use it your nose will seize up worse than ever.

Aspirin and Paracetamol

Method: As usual read the label on the bottle for dosage and frequency.

How they work: They reduce body temperature and curb the pain of sore throats and headaches. Taking more than the prescribed dose is futile as well as dangerous.

Pros and Cons: They're convenient. But they won't shorten a cold's duration, and long-term use of aspirin has been shown to make noses run.

Vitamin C (Ascorbic Acid)

Method: Taken in soluble, sometimes effervescent tablets from the chemist's. You'll need at least five grams per day, but because it tends to escape in the urine, you'll need to take it at regular intervals. There's not enough natural vitamin C in fruit or vegetables to affect colds.

How it works: see 'Colds & Vitamin C', page 51.

Pros and Cons: Taken in these quantities, vitamin C tablets are quite expensive. And for every doctor who believes vitamin C works against colds, there's one who doesn't.

Zinc

Method: Tablets from the chemist.

How it works: see 'Colds & Zinc', page 55.

Pros and Cons: Even more expensive than vitamin C. Zinc has seemed to shorten colds among volunteers in scientific tests, but results in the outside world can't be guaranteed.

Reducing Anxiety and Stress

Method: Undertake relaxation regimes, take more exercise, especially outdoors, delegate more at the office, take more holidays.

How it works: The state of mind is linked to the immune system. Clinical tests show that people under stress are twice as likely to catch a cold.

Pros and Cons: Suddenly relaxing (for instance, taking a very lazy holiday) after a period of intense activity often brings on a cold.

A Clean Mouth

Method: Brush the teeth vigorously five times a day. Gargle with tap water often, taking care to spit it all out.

How it works: The swilling action may flush out viruses in the throat and crevices in the teeth. And even if it doesn't get to them, it will almost certainly reduce secondary bacteria.

Pros and Cons: It may keep dental decay at bay, but frequent swilling out is time-consuming. And such is the reproductive power of viruses that the effect on your cold will be marginal.

How To Tell Colds From Flu

'Ye can call it influenza if ye like,' said Mrs
Machin. 'There was no influenza in my young
days. We called a cold a cold.'
The Card, Arnold Bennett (1867–1931)

Cold viruses and influenza viruses belong to completely
different families. But as it is often hard to tell a severe cold
from flu, it's useful to know how to tell them apart. There are
perhaps 300 cold viruses but only three basic strains of flu.

Influenza occurs much less often than colds. While cold
bugs lurk around every corner, flu viruses sometimes
disappear for years on end. When it occurs, it's usually as a
winter epidemic. How flu viruses manage suddenly to infect
large areas of the earth at more or less the same time is one of
the major medical mysteries. The viruses seem to travel
almost as fast as light.

The Main Differences

Cold viruses attack the nose and upper parts of the throat.
Although flu goes only for the throat, it causes muscle pain
all over the body and this is accompanied by fever and a
powerful, throbbing headache.

A cold can also cause aching limbs and a headache, but
these aren't the most common symptoms and they're milder.
Colds may also raise your temperature, but not very often
and rarely above 37.8°C (100°F). A flu temperature may reach

39.4°C (103°F), sometimes even more, especially among children.

The symptoms of flu strike more suddenly than those of a cold. There's sometimes a nose bleed and a painful dry cough which produces only a little phlegm.

A reliable way to tell flu from a cold is the effect it has on the eyes. During a cold the eyes may stream. But in flu, the eyeballs ache and the patient becomes intolerant of bright light.

Cold sufferers sometimes decide to stay in bed. Flu victims have no choice. They feel very groggy indeed and it hurts when they move about.

Influenza normally lasts just four days, only about half as long as a typical cold. But severe cases can keep patients bedridden for a fortnight. Unlike a cold, which usually ends with a feeling of well-being or relief, flu sufferers often feel weak and lethargic for up to six weeks.

Complications

In the great flu epidemic of 1918–19, 20 million people died worldwide, not from the flu itself but from follow-up diseases, mainly pneumonia and bronchitis.

Serious bouts of flu may also affect the heart. A doctor would look for signs of this in bluish colouring of the lips and mouth.

Although your doctor can do little to alleviate flu symptoms, be sure to consult him or her if your illness lasts more than four days, in case some additional, and possibly more serious infection has taken hold.

Vaccination

You cannot be immunized against a cold, but you can be against flu. It's claimed that eight out of 10 vaccinated people won't catch it, while the other two will suffer only mild symptoms. Dying of any disease precipitated by flu is extremely rare after vaccination has taken place.

You need to be inoculated every year because the viruses have the ability to change slightly from year to year. They do this by altering their protein shell just enough to provide a defence against our antibodies. Don't have a flu jab if you're allergic to eggs – they are used in the production of some vaccines.

A Flu 'Cure'

A drug called amantidine alleviates the symptoms of one of the major flu strains, Beijing flu, by attacking the virus. And although it is ineffective against the other strains, it gives hope that colds, too, may eventually be eradicated by anti-viral drugs.

Pull the Other One!

Let's start with a well-respected maxim: 'Feed a cold and starve a fever.' It's sufficient to say that many people get it the wrong way round and that, either way, it has no basis in scientific fact.

Presumably the fever referred to here is the one caused by influenza. As it happens, the diet to treat both colds and flu is the same: light meals of nutritious fare (no junk food) and plenty of liquids.

The Garlic Cure

Garlic, a most excellent bringer-out of flavours in many fine foods, has a variety of bogus curative virtues attached to it. Many people are convinced it keeps colds at bay; some even believe it helps prevent TB. There's no good evidence to support either belief.

Even dafter is the time-honoured garlic cure for sore throats. Sufferers are advised to crush it, mix it with goose grease, and rub it into the soles of the feet. Believe me, all you will get is smelly feet.

Curry

It's quite widely believed that a specially supercharged vindaloo is just the thing for a cold, presumably on the grounds that the heat generated will knock the viruses for six. Don't bother – the most likely result will be a stomach ache, especially if you're not used to Indian food.

A Hot Bath

This is based on the misconception that you can 'sweat-out' a cold – that perspiration oozing from our pores carries the germs with it, so ridding the body of invaders. It can't work. Cold bugs inhabit only the nose and throat.

The hot bath myth is all part of the larger misapprehension that if chilly weather causes colds (it doesn't), a hot environment should reverse the process (it won't). This is the only possible explanation for the plainly daft belief that a foot bath will keep colds at bay. The final lunacy is to add mustard to the water.

The Open Window

The woolly thinking here is that your bedroom becomes crowded with cold germs during the night and that keeping the window and curtains open will allow the viruses to fly away. This is bunkum. Fresh air from an open window may make your laboured breathing easier if you live by the sea or in the countryside. But polluted city air will do more harm than good.

More Maxims

* 'Don't go out without a hat on.' This may have some benefit for people who already have a cold. The body needs to keep its temperature up to fight the virus and 40 per cent of bodily heat loss is through the head. But going hatless won't stop you getting a cold in the first place.
* 'Don't go out with your hair wet.' This makes you pretty shivery, but it won't cause a cold.
* 'Evacuate your bowels three times a day.' This is supposed to improve your natural resistance, though it's difficult to know how. It will undoubtledly relieve you of constipation

– but cold viruses are not found in the alimentary canal.
* 'Harden your resistance with cold baths.' This comes into the same category as scorning overcoats or scarves, and going for cross-country runs in freezing weather. Unfortunately, to the cold virus, the fitness freak is just as soft a touch as a couch potato. Hardening off may work for plants, but there's no evidence that it protects humans against colds. But don't discourage members of your family from fitness training if they want to do it. Apart from anything else, it will make them feel the cold less – with beneficial effects on your central heating bills!

The Ice Cure

This is supposed to bring out hidden illnesses lurking in the body. And although it's admitted that the treatment might engender cold symptoms you didn't have before, it's claimed that you'll get fewer coughs, blockages and sore throats in the future.

The method is to fold a thick towel in half to make a square. Put a dozen ice cubes in the middle. Fold the four corners upwards and towards each other over the ice. Then get into bed, lying on another towel.

Place the freezing bundle over your stomach and nether regions. The thickly folded corners should be on top of the towel to stop your sheets getting soggy. As the ice melts the towel will become freezing cold. You have to sleep in this position for three hours.

Advocaters of this cure say that while you sleep the body sends blood to the cold area to warm it. Then the blood returns to the heart and lungs, taking impurities and poisons with it.

It's hard to see how this is supposed to put down any viruses. And as you're supposed to take this ice-bath every four days for several weeks, you might well prefer to suffer a heavy cold than this regime of nocturnal torture.

Some Higher Lunacies

So far most of the nostrums we've described in this chapter are based on more or less understandable premises, however crazy. The following, however, are just plain barking – and, moreover, are grounded in the doleful philosophy that cures, to be effective, must be painful or nauseating, and preferably both.

1. Tie a very well-used sock around your neck until the affliction goes away. The more noisome the sock, the greater its healing powers.
2. Put grated nutmeg in both shoes.
3. Peel an orange, roll up the rind, and stick a roll in each nostril.
4. Take bread and milk before bed.
5. Smear soap up your nose.
6. Take off all your clothes and stand in front of a draught for 10 minutes a day.
7. Rub methylated spirits into a bald head.
8. Grow a moustache right up to the nostrils.
9. Step over cracks in pavements.
10. Stand on your head under water.
11. Do *not* blow your nose.
12. Strap a bag of onions on your back. Or go to bed with chopped onions in your socks.

Colds: A History

I have caught
An everlasting cold,
I have lost my voice,
Most irrecoverably.
The White Devil,
by John Webster (1580–1625)

When humans first walked the earth they must have had a bleak and dangerous time of it, but at least they didn't suffer from colds. Neither, despite their somewhat skimpy attire, did Adam and Eve. Viruses can only live in large human communities. With a small group living in a cave, such gregarious viruses would have had nowhere to go once the cave-dwellers' immunity had repelled them.

In that case, how did cold viruses suddenly appear? Well, once man began to live in large tribal groups or in the early cities, rhinoviruses and the rest would have had a chance to evolve from other bugs. Perhaps they began in our intestines, or possibly they originated as an affliction of other animals but gradually found man a more accommodating host and over a period of time evolved to become specific to humans.

Some have suggested that cold viruses were brought to earth by crashing asteroids. There's no particular reason to believe this, although traces of nucleic acid, one of the chemicals basic to living organisms, have been found in these visitors from space.

First Recorded Cold?

One of the earliest colds on record befell Jacob, grandson of Abraham and son of Isaac. Around 2,000 BC, Jacob was fleeing from the wrath of his older twin Esau, whom he'd tried to usurp as heir to the family's wealth.

Alone in the desert, he fell prey to chills and a fever. This cold, if it was one, may have fulfilled Divine purpose. The future patriarch fell into an exhausted sleep and had his vision of 'Jacob's Ladder'. Angels were moving up and down this flimsy route to heaven, symbolizing God's accessibility to humankind.

Jacob's cold is mentioned not in the Bible, but is written up in the *Book of the Parsees* (an ancient religious sect, originally from Persia and now found in India.)

A New Testament Streamer?

In three of the four gospels there's an account of Simon Peter's mother-in-law coming down with what sounds like a feverish cold. In one of the first of his miracles, Jesus touches her hand 'and she arose and was able to minister to them'.

An Epic Cure

Serenus Sammonicus, a noted physician in classical Roman times, advocated that citizens who wanted to rid themselves of chills and shivers should sleep with a passage from Homer's *Iliad* under their heads. Those wishing to try this cure should note that only Book IV of Homer's epic will do. This passage tells of the duel between the Spartan King Menelaos (husband of Helen, whom the Trojans had kidnapped) and one of the Trojan champions. It is agreed that if Menelaos wins, the city of Troy will be surrendered to the besieging Greek armies. At the end of the duel, the judge, Agamemnon – who is not only the Greek commander in chief but Menelaos's brother – pronounces Menelaos the winner.

One of the Trojan commanders, Pandoros, infuriated by Agamemnon's verdict, grievously wounds Menelaos, whose life is saved by the skill of Machaon, the Greeks' military surgeon. It is this almost miraculous recovery that persuaded Serenus of the book's curative properties. Be that as it may, you cannot get the *Iliad* on the National Health.

Romans Grasp the Nettle

The Roman invaders of Britain, most of whose soldiers were used to Mediterranean climes, soon realized they needed medicines to combat the effects of our damp and chilly climate on their forces. They took the advice of the Greek physician Pedanios Dioscorides, who believed that nettles contained substances that could cure many ailments, including the common cold. Dioscorides studied hundreds of plants and described their medicinal properties in his *Materia Medica* (AD 77–8), which was to remain a standard medical book for 1500 years.

To help stave off the great British cold and rheumatism, the Romans brought nettle seeds across the Channel to plant in our soil. And since that time there has been a widespread belief that an infusion of nettles heats the blood and cures a sore throat. What is certain is that the relentless spread of nettles every year is calculated to heat the blood of British gardeners, however attractive they may be to butterflies.

Old English Cures

In the Middle Ages many physicians believed that secretions from the nose during a streamer originated in the brain, finding their way into the nose through small holes.

In 1672 Dr Richard Lower, in a treatise entitled *De Catarrhis*, scotched the oozing brain theory, only to replace it with another equally dotty. He asserted that a runny nose was caused by blocked pores in the skin, which became bunged up in cold weather. When this happened, waste products of the blood could not get out through perspiration ducts and instead congregated in glands around the nose and the throat. Eventually they dripped out.

Other medical books of the time advised patients not to drink *anything* for three or four days. This was expected to dry up a runny nose – which no doubt it would after the patient had died of dehydration.

Another treatment was that good old stand-by, bleeding, in which a vein was opened up in the forearm twice a day supposedly to allow the illness to escape from the body.

Cooks and Colds

Early cookery books as well as herbals invariably included information on the medicinal properties of culinary plants and instructions for making dishes to cure everyday complaints.

Tasty cold recipes in the 17th century included a mixture of red wine, rose leaves and the peelings of a pomegranate. Or you could have barley water with mulberry syrup and roses. And Elinor Fettiplace's *Receipt Book* of 1604 offered this eggnog 'For a Great Cold':

'Take the yolk of an egg, and one spoonful of aqua vitae, and four spoonfuls of goats or cowe milk, hot from the cow, beat it all together, and then drink it fasting late at night.'

Cooks in the great houses of that time also knew how to make coughdrops, syrups and gargling concoctions for sore throats.

The Red Indian Tragedy

Meanwhile, a human disaster was unfolding in North America, where settlers from Europe were making contact with the local Indian peoples – and passing on all the common European diseases.

Even the common cold proved fatal to the Amerindians, who had been isolated from the viruses and had built up no immunity. The infections quickly opened the way to more serious illnesses like pneumonia, and the result was inevitable. While thousands of native Americans met their deaths from the guns of the white man, hundreds of thousands were killed by his diseases.

Pass It On!

The fact that people caught colds from each other was surprisingly slow to catch on. The accepted wisdom was that chilling caused by draughts, icy rooms and wet feet was the only culprit. It was recognized that other diseases, such as bubonic plague, appeared to spread from one person to another. Yet even when there were clear indications that colds were also infectious, few people would accept the evidence.

In Boswell's *Life of Samuel Johnson* (1791) we read of the natives of the lonely isle of St Kilda coming down with colds after a ship sailed into the harbour. Boswell ascribed this mini-epidemic not to the wheezy ship's crew but to the weather. You could not land a vessel at this island in the Outer Hebrides unless the wind was in the north-east, and that particular wind – Boswell reasoned – was uncomfortably chilly and therefore a bringer of colds.

The Mysteries of Immunity

No serious research into the mystery of colds was done until the 1860s when the French chemist Louis Pasteur, studying the fermentation process, laid the foundations for the modern sciences of bacteriology and immunology. After that a host of diseases such as cholera, typhoid and tuberculosis were each found to be caused by a specific bacterium.

At the turn of the century there was a new twist. In 1899 a German military surgeon, Friedrich Löffler, discovered that foot-and-mouth disease was caused by some unknown organism, much smaller than bacteria, which passed through an ultra-fine sieve that intercepted bacteria without fail.

Then in 1914, Dr Walther Kruse from Leipzig, Germany, took mucus from the dripping nose of his assistant and diluted it with water. He passed the liquid through a filter fine enough to trap any organism known at that time. Afterwards, he swabbed the nostrils of a dozen colleagues with this liquid. Four of them developed colds. He deduced, correctly, that colds are caused by a virus.

The Common Cold Research Unit

During World War II the Allies made plans to combat the outbreak of epidemics. The American Red Cross and Harvard University sent over 100 medical researchers to Britain to help deal with any outbreaks. A number of pre-fab laboratories were also flown over from the United States. These were set up on Salisbury Plain in Wiltshire.

The epidemics never happened, so the US Army Medical Corps used the centre for research into various diseases. At the war's end, the unit was handed over to the Ministry of Health. In 1946 the Medical Research Council moved in. The Common Cold Research Unit was formed and asked for volunteers to help them in their search for a cure for the cold.

In 1992, after 46 years, the British government refused to fund the unit any longer, and it closed without having found a complete cure. Nonetheless, its founder, Sir Christopher Andrews, and his colleagues discovered a great deal about cold viruses and laid to rest a few myths. Yet the fact remains that today there is no permanent centre devoted solely to research into this scourge.

Going Off Sick

Saying you're not coming into work because of a cold never gains you much sympathy. You can tell that by the frosty voice of the boss when you call in.

This is one reason why so many cold sufferers claim to have flu. But, as everyone knows, this convinces nobody. A more subtle approach is called for:

* The afternoon before you intend to stay off work, complain gently about your sore throat and cough a lot. Go to the toilets and rub your nose to redden it slightly. There's no need to overdo this for colleagues to expect your absence the next day.
* Get someone else – like your husband, mum or flatmate – to call the office on your behalf. This way you will appear more incapacitated.
* If there's no one else to make the call, do a lot of shouting just before you dial. This will make you hoarse. Distancing yourself at least five inches from the phone will also make you sound particularly fragile.
* Never call the night before to say you won't be coming in. This appears too premeditated. The best time is 15 minutes after your starting time, when the office is already beginning to suspect you might not make it.
* If you think your employer won't accept a cold as a valid reason, try gastric flu (perceived to be more incapacitating than ordinary flu) or even a slipped disc.
* Never give an estimated time when you might be back.

Cough a lot

Employees usually get held to guesses like this.
* Never venture outside if you're not at work because of a cold. Remember Howard's Law: someone will always spot you.

A Question of Conscience

Very often a patient kept at home by a cold is pestered by a still small voice saying he or she should really be at work. This nuisance call can occur as often as every half-hour.

The best way to silence this voice is to remember:
* The minimal time you've had off during your career.
* That your absence will prevent your colleagues going down with the same bug.
* How much more efficient you'll be once you've shaken the thing off.
* The ridiculously small salary you're paid.
* The immense amount of time others take off for long lunches and golf.
* How being sacked from such a tedious job wouldn't be the end of the world.
* How much your absence will make your colleagues realize your talents.

When To Return After a Cold

The correct policy is always to go back a day after you feel fit enough to. Or two days if it was a particularly bad bout. This is by way of a compensatory treat for all the misery you've been through.

It's not advisable to have just one or two days off with a cold. This gives an impression that your disability wasn't serious enough to merit *any* time off at all. At least a week is the rule.

Celebrity Colds

Everytime I see dancing girls it strikes me that at least one just might have a severe cold that will be aggravated by stage fright and lack of sleep.

All that energy demanded for the routine will be diverted away from their defence systems so the viruses will be multiplying like crazy. Yet they have to turn up, to keep smiling; the show must go on.

It's the same for an actor who must hide a cold. James Bond with a streaming red nose simply isn't acceptable. John le Carré never wrote a story turned into a film called *The Spy Who Came in with a Cold*.

Whereas the rest of us can usually slow down, performers and VIPs must carry on. It's to these martyrs that this chapter is respectfully dedicated.

Singing in the Rain

During the filming of the storm-lashed street scene in this famous musical, its star was suffering from a severe cold. It says a lot for Gene Kelly's legendary professionalism and the fact that his rain-washed face hid the streaming nose, that he managed to pull it off without anyone knowing he was ill. The scenes where water from broken guttering plummets down his neck and he stamps around in puddles must have been particularly unpleasant.

Softening up the jury

Buddy Holly and the Big Bopper

Early in 1959, pop legend Buddy Holly starred in a touring rock 'n' roll show called the 'Winter Dance Party'. Also on the bill were J P Richardson, known as The Big Bopper, and 17-year-old Ritchie Valens. The Big Bopper was enjoying a million-selling hit with 'Chantilly Lace', one of the all-time rock 'n' roll classics.

In February the show played to an audience in Clear Lake, Iowa. The next day it was due in Minnesota. To avoid a long coach trip, Buddy Holly hired a small plane to take himself and two of his backing group to the new venue.

Big Bopper had caught a cold and didn't think an overnight ride on a draughty bus would make him feel any better. So he persuaded one of Buddy's group, Waylon Jennings, to give up his seat on the plane. Ritchie Valens also arranged a similar swap. Big Bopper's cold proved fatal. The plane with its 21-year-old pilot crashed. There were no survivors.

The Queen of Colds

Probably the most famous speech our present Queen ever made was delivered under the influence of a shocking cold.

She was already nursing a corker when a large part of Windsor Castle went up in flames in November 1992. The fumes from the still smouldering castle could hardly have helped matters.

A few days later, at a lunch in Guildhall to celebrate the fortieth year of her reign, the smoke's abrasive effect took its toll. As a result, the now legendary Annus Horribilis speech was hardly heard.

The Queen's year had indeed been grim. Apart from the Windsor blaze, the Duke and Duchess of York announced their separation in March, Princess Anne had filed for divorce from Captain Mark Phillips in April, the book *Diana, Her True Story* came out in June, the *Mirror* published intimate pictures of Fergie in August and, in Dresden in

October, two eggs were thrown at the Queen's car. The speech called for critics to show a 'touch of gentleness, good humour and understanding'. It was finely balanced to shame the press into not making a meal of royal disasters in the future, while not appearing to be fishing for public sympathy.

But the squeaky throat had an unfortunate effect: the Queen cut a sadder more put-upon figure at Guildhall than she intended.

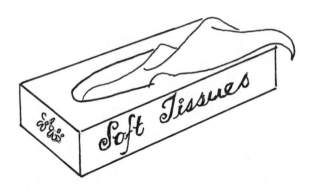

Colds and the Seasons

Wheear as tha bin Ah saw thee?
On Ilkley Moor baht at
Wheear as tha bin sin Ah saw thee?
On Ilkley Moor baht at.

Tha'll go 'n catch thee deeath o' cowld,
On Ilkley Moor baht at
Tha'll go 'n catch thee deeath o' cowld
On Ilkley Moor baht at.

Then we'll have to bury thee
On Ilkley Moor baht at,
Then we'll have to bury thee
On Ilkley Moor baht at.

The words of the old Yorkshire song reflected what everyone 'knew': that leaving your fireside to venture out on a freezing day without a woolly hat (and other warm clothes) would inevitably result in a cold. If you lingered in a draught, took a cold bath or stepped from the fireside into an icy backyard you were asking for it. And very seriously was the advice taken, because colds in those days posed a much more serious threat than they do now: they could turn into lethal pneumonia or fatally aggravate the common scourge of tuberculosis.

If you caught a cold, you went straight to bed. It was dangerous not to.

What Do We Think Now?

My father always made me wash my feet in hot water to raise their temperature if they were dampened in a snowball fight or a puddle-stamping contest. The idea was to heat them up again and prevent a cold. He still believes this.

In an unscientific survey for this book, I asked 200 people in Doncaster if they thought wet feet or going out in appalling weather could start a cold. More than half (111) thought that low temperatures and damp clothing caused colds. Yet most doctors now insist that you can never blame the climate or wet feet.

Are they right to be so dogmatic? There's evidence that it's not quite as simple as that.

A Winter's Tale

In whatever country surveys have been carried out, and they include Jamaica, the United States and Britain, the number of colds rises steeply in autumn and winter. They're uncommon in July, but in August they start to creep up again. Interestingly, researchers have found that the incidence of bunged up noses peaks and falls at least three times during autumn and winter.

In temperate climates like ours, the highest number of respiratory infections come in October. After this, most of us stay snuffle-free until Christmas, when the viruses attack again. Then there's a lull before a final outbreak in March.

The explanations often given for these periods of extra-viral activity sound convincing – at first.

The Late August/September Cold

Children pick up a varied set of viruses at the seaside and other new places during their summer holidays. They return to school in September and pass on these new bugs to their classmates. At home these infections are passed on to parents, who relay them in shops and offices to the neighbourhood at large.

The Christmas Cold

Just before Christmas the body is worn out by shopping, parties and general anxiety. We find it hard to summon the extra energy to cope with infections waiting in the wings. We also mix more with strangers as we push through crowded stores.

Cold symptoms often start when tension suddenly dissipates. This could be on Christmas Day, when the panic shopping has been finally left behind. And elderly people living on their own suddenly find themselves in the company of virus-toting young relatives at family get-togethers.

The March Cold

In this month, the argument goes, the immunity we gained after the rush of early and mid-winter colds begins to wear off. Invading viruses have a clearer field.

Are these seasonal factors really significant enough to cause epidemics of colds? Or is the explanation much simpler – that chilly weather itself triggers the contagions.

The Virus Within

One possible explanation of why we suffer more colds when the temperature falls is to be found in the 'sleeping virus' theory. This argues that, as well as picking up cold bugs from the air around us, we already have some dormant cold viruses in residence inside us.

Sudden changes in the weather might trigger these sluggish specks into action, attacking the cells in the mucous membrane and multiplying furiously. Another cold epidemic is set in train. The idea of dormant germs is supported by the frequent discovery of rhinoviruses in the nasal secretions of people with no cold symptoms. Further support comes in the

case of another unrelated virus, *Herpes simplex*, which causes
cold sores. This pest has no effect on the body until we
develop a cold. Then the virus causes blisters to form on the
lips and eventually to turn into scabs. *Herpes simplex* may be
present but inactive in the body for several years, and it is
possible that cold viruses can behave in the same way.

The Quarantine Theory

If Robinson Crusoe had a drippy nose when he was
shipwrecked on to his island (and sailors confined together
on a ship are notoriously susceptible), it would soon have
run its course. And as there was no one to give him a new
infection, he would then have remained cold-free – at least
until Friday came along.

By the same reasoning, if everyone on earth locked
themselves alone in a room for two weeks at the same time,
no common cold viruses could survive and the scourge
would vanish forever. At least, it would unless the dormant
virus theory turns out to be sound. If people really can
harbour viruses for long periods before they erupt into colds,
mass quarantine of the entire population would not
eradicate the viruses but only slow them down for a while.

Cold and Cold Viruses

Another reason why colds are most prevalent in winter may
be that windows are more often shut at this time of the year,
allowing more viruses to accumulate in the air. But even this
cannot fully explain the huge surge in December colds.

So it could be that viruses simply do better if colder air
finds its way into your nose, or that cool weather causes the
nose to produce more secretions, which help bugs to get
about more, both in the nose and also outside it, where they
would infect more people. And so, while it is true that cold
weather, as such, is not the cause of colds, it does seem that
colds and cold weather do go together.

Alternative Treatments

Fringe, or alternative, medicine covers an enormous range of theory and practices which are not always recognized by most conventionally trained doctors or the medical profession as a whole. In a few cases, the rejection, and even ridicule, of fringe practices is justified. But it is now being increasingly realized that some of these practices have a lot going for them.

One sign of this change of attitude is that many popular medical reference books now contain advice not only from conventional doctors but also from other experts who would once have been regarded as faith healers or quacks. In this chapter we have a brief look at some 'alternative' approaches to the common cold.

Herbalism

Herbalists claim to reduce symptoms slowly but surely. They set more store than GPs in building up long-term resistance, so that you have fewer and milder colds. Make a point of consulting only an experienced herbalist because even herbs may have side effects.

Extracts of the following herbs commonly recommended for colds are available from herbalists and health stores.
* **Catmint** Controls nasal congestion and stress; improves circulation.
* **Elderflower** Reduces catarrh. Helps keep the temperature normal.

* **Camomile** Helps to prevent high temperatures; soothes inflammation of the mucous membrane. Good for sore throats.
* **Hyssop** Helps to stop coughing.

The easy way to take herbal medicines is in the form of tablets or granules. Some can be bought as capsules which dissolve in the stomach, so cutting the risk of tainted breath. But herbs are cheaper in their natural or dried state.

Elderflowers, fresh or dried, are best made into a tea. Steep them in boiling water for 15 minutes, strain and drink, preferably just before going to bed. Rose hip tea is also recommended because of its vitamin C content.

Homoeopathy

This branch of alternative medicine advocates taking substances which, in a healthy person, would cause the same symptoms as the disease, though in a milder form. This, it's argued, builds up immunity.

For a cold, a homoeopath might recommend a remedy called Pulsatilla. This is believed to be effective on colds which begin with swollen glands and produce a lot of mucus and perspiration. The treatment might be a substance called a nosode, which is prepared from diseased lung tissue. It works like a delayed vaccination, being given after and not before the cold. The dose would be gradually increased and still taken after the cold's disappearance to build up defences against further bouts.

Acupuncture

The ancient Chinese believed that the cold is caused by a Wind-Cold or a Wind-Heat. These gusts blow away the Qi on the surface of the head and neck. (The Qi can be roughly translated as the body's natural resistance.)

Acupuncture as a way of strengthening the Qi in order to resist colds is common in China. In Britain, where the treatment can be expensive, acupuncture is rarely used for relatively short-lived afflictions. However, if you suffer frequent and severe colds every year, you might feel acupuncture would be worthwhile.

An acupuncturist would insert his needles above the lungs, bladder, spleen and stomach in order to scatter phlegm and strengthen the lungs against infection. Special massage of the arms, chest and back is used between treatments. There is also a 'cold diet' to cut down on 'damp-producing' foods. Treatments to prevent a recurrence of colds are carried out for some months afterwards, and for up to two years for someone who is particularly prone to infection.

Osteopathy

Osteopaths believe that diseases of many kinds are due mainly to deformation of the skeleton, and practical osteopathy is primarily concerned with manipulation of the joints, where disorders of the nervous system and blood circulation system may occur.

Osteopathy places emphasis on the whole person, rather than the idea of treating the complaint locally. The method does not pretend to be the answer to any single episode, but aims to make a sufferer more resilient to the complaint in general.

Osteopaths regard bunged up noses, sore throats and coughs as encouraging symptoms, helping the system to eliminate harmful waste. They see colds as a useful warning sign of an unhealthy body, perhaps caused by poor diet and lack of exercise.

A qualified osteopath would begin by changing the diet of his patient. Dairy products and fatty dishes such as egg and chips would be banned. These foods are thought to increase catarrh. Often the treatment begins with a fast. Then, after a day or two, the patient would be fed on nourishing foods only.

Chiropractic

This branch of alternative medicine seeks to cure many common health problems by paying attention to posture, the back, the neck and particularly the spine. It would be pointless embarking on such treatment for one cold, but it would be of benefit if you're never free of them.

The practitioner will check the spine for any abnormalities, and will manipulate it to correct them. It could take several visits. The aim is to improve overall health and strengthen the body's resistance to colds.

Conclusion

The sensible advice is that, if you spend a large part of your life dogged by colds and you have the money, to go and see an alternative specialist. After all, your GP can't do much to help. But try some of the other remedies in this book first.

The Sneeze Button

The sneeze is the cold bug's most efficient way of getting about. A sneeze will propel virus-crammed water droplets at a speed of more than 100 miles an hour, and anyone within 30 feet of the sneezer is liable to be infected. So imagine what damage may be done by a sneezer on a crowded bus.

Sneezing is an involuntary action the body takes to get rid of any alien bits and pieces which get sucked into the nasal passages. It prevents this foreign matter from piling into and abrading the sensitive tissues of the lungs. We sneeze during a cold but not because the nasal passages are reacting to viruses. Sensitive though these channels are, they can't detect the undetectable.

The Mechanics of Sneezing

There's more to this reflex action than you might think. It involves five different processes within a few seconds.

* The chest muscles force the ribs apart and contract the diaphragm, the muscular wall between the lungs and the stomach. This action rapidly sucks 2.5 litres (more than 150 cubic inches) of air into the lungs.
* The windpipe closes, trapping this extra air.
* The muscles of the stomach force it upwards, against the diaphragm. At the same time, chest muscles contract, increasing the air pressure in the lungs.
* Now the windpipe snaps open and the pressurized air explodes out.

* Muscles at the back of the nasal channels contract, so that most of the air shoots out through the nostrils rather than the mouth.

A Fatal Pleasure?

Sneezing for most of us is a decidedly pleasurable experience. It not only feels liberating, but it achieves a considerable effect for very little effort – something which always appeals to us. This is why toddlers will beam at you after an aa-tishoo!

Yet sneezing is perhaps the nearest a healthy person comes to death. While we do it, the heart stops beating, we cease breathing and we can't see a thing. Sneezers should always face directly forward. It's been known for people who let forth while twisting their necks sideways to suffer a slipped disc.

The Sneeze Effect

As we've seen, during a cold there's plenty of extra mucus formed in the nose. Foreign bodies stick to the mucus, and the hurricane of a sneeze shoots the top layer into the atmosphere.

The resulting cloud is more or less invisible. You may see a few of the larger blobs of mucus, but these are not as dangerous as the smaller, lighter droplets. These hang about in the air, heaving with viruses, as if waiting to colonize any noses that happen to pass.

For the sneezer, however, there are benefits. He can, of course, breathe more easily for some time afterwards, and the uncomfortable general sensation of a cold will leave him for at least 10 minutes.

Your body, if not your conscience, is quite unconcerned about passing on cold viruses to other people. A sneeze is simply the body's most efficient way of giving the bugs the boot.

When a Sneeze is Most Infectious

The infectiousness of a sneeze depends on the concentration of viruses in the droplets expelled. At the start of a cold the concentration will be high. After a few days, antibodies will have killed a proportion of viruses in the mucus, so that the number of bugs in a sneeze cloud is depleted.

It's worth noting that, if the theory of dormant cold viruses is correct (see page 97), it is possible to sneeze cold germs on to someone else even though you have no reason to suppose you are infected. Indeed, sneezing may be the only indication that you are harbouring cold viruses.

Reducing the Damage

Those who try for a noise record every time they sneeze are merely show-offs. It's perfectly possible to convert a full-blown example into a polite 'choo'.

Hay-fever sufferers must learn how to do this or they may eventually collapse due to the energy expended by a continuous stream of full-blown sneezes. I once interviewed for radio a teenager suffering from an allergy who sneezed every few seconds of her life. Of necessity she had to make the sneeze as gentle and indiscernible as possible. She learned to do this to great effect, her sneezes hardly interrupting her conversation.

It's possible to suppress a sneeze completely. If you suddenly think of something unpleasing, such as an acutely embarrassing or painful experience, the seemingly inexorable progress towards a sneeze may be halted, at least for a while. Other ways to stifle a sneeze are:

* Hold your breath
* Pinch your nose on both sides about half-way down, where the bone ends.
* Touch the roof of your mouth with the top of your tongue.
* Blow your nose instead.

If you feel a sneeze is unavoidable, whip out your handkerchief and cover your nose and mouth. Then keep the handkerchief away from other objects or people, as the viruses will thrive in your dampened hankie.

Stopping Somebody Else's Sneeze

The cartoonist's way of stopping a sneezer in his tracks by placing the first finger horizontally just under his nose at the crucial moment may actually work – merely because the shock of this unexpected action drags his attention way from the business of sneezing. Bursting a paper bag behind his back could have the same result.

'Bless You!'

This is one of the oldest responses to a sneeze still practised today. The Greek philosopher Aristotle (384–22 BC) wrote that his countrymen were terrified of a sneeze because it was seen as an early symptom of plague. If you sneezed in the company of your friends, they would hurriedly intone 'Zeus be with you' and leave without delay. The ancient Romans, too, greeted a sneeze with the words 'Absit omen' (roughly, 'May evil be absent').

The idea that sneezing is an ill-omen was widespread for centuries in Persia, India, Africa and Sweden.

The 19th century American poet Longfellow, author of *Hiawatha*, was fascinated by sneezing. He reported that when the Spanish Conquistadors first landed in Florida and one of them sneezed, the alarmed locals lifted up their arms as one and implored the sun to avert the ill-omen.

The first use of the words 'God bless you!' in response to a sneeze are attributed to St Gregory (AD 240–332), the Apostle of Armenia, who is said to have given the benediction to sneezers during a pestilence.

Other Sneezing Superstitions

Not all the superstitions associate sneezing with illness or misfortune. In Scotland, it's thought that a baby is under the spell of fairies until the first time it sneezes, suggesting there are no colds in Fairyland.

In the United States it used to be said that people who sneeze while in conversation are telling the truth. Salesmen in rural areas often pretended to sneeze to clinch a deal. And Americans who nearly but not quite sneeze know that they have a secret admirer somewhere.

Some Italians believe that your soul leaves your body if you rattle the crockery with a sneeze, and that it can be brought back only if someone implores Divine help.

A Jewish superstition holds that anyone sneezing during a discussion about somebody's death will bring bad luck on everyone present – unless someone quickly pulls his ear while intoning 'They in their world, we in ours.'

Fake Colds

Many people suffer runny noses, sore throats, sneezes and other symptoms which prove not to have been colds at all. Let's look at some of these cold mimics.

Allergies

A 'cold' occurring between May and August, when the pollen count is high, should be treated with suspicion – it could be due to an allergy. The symptoms are so similar they might fool anyone and even if you've never been troubled before, hay-fever can suddenly strike.

If you look up the typical symptoms of any allergy you'll find fever, headache, a sore throat, streaming eyes and a blocked nose. Sounds familiar? Among everyday substances that may cause allergic reactions are tea, car-exhaust fumes and bread. If your 'cold' disappears during the day and bounces back at night you may be sensitive to feathers in your pillow or dust in the bedding. House mites and mould on old stonework are other common culprits which can set you off.

The reason allergies and colds share symptoms is that antibodies react to all sorts of invaders in the same way as they do to viruses. Tiny specks can be sucked into our bodies from many substances. Some we will tolerate without their triggering our defence system; others we won't.

In order to deal with allergens, the troublesome particles which cause allergies, the body produces a chemical called histamine (see page 40), which produces the allergic reactions. Drugs called antihistamines are useful for countering this problem among sufferers from hay-fever and other allergies. But some tests show antihistamines are not as effective in reducing congestion caused by colds.

There's a theory that an individual catching a lot of colds is less likely to suffer hay-fever. The reasoning is that all those viral attacks give frequent practical training to the body's defence system in how to do its job properly. So the antibodies are not so likely to confuse specks of pollen and other allergens for rhinoviruses.

Sick-Building Syndrome

Modern buildings make many office workers feel ill runny noses, headaches and low-grade fever being typical symptoms. The problems may be due to air-conditioning systems which help to circulate all sorts of irritating particles. Or they may be caused by fumes given off by man made materials. If you work in an office block and suffer these symptoms but perk up at the week-end, you could well be a victim of sick-building syndrome.

Central Heating

This dries up the atmosphere. The throat, which is used to dampish conditions, becomes irritated when this unnaturally dry air passes down it. The nose does its best to moisturize the incoming air, but it can't cope.

A scratchy throat is produced which feels like the onset of a cold. The discomfort disappears, however, when the heating is turned off, or you go outside. Don't get alarmed if this recovery doesn't happen immediately: your throat may need a little more time to recover. The problem can be eliminated by putting a wet towel over the nearest radiator, or by occasionally boiling a kettle of water for a minute or so. Or you can install a purpose-made humidifier.

I often used to fear I was starting a stinker towards the end of a long car journey. I know now that it was probably the effect of the car heater pushing out dry, warm air. (The problem was compounded by the fact that my car had a heater which wouldn't switch off.) New cars, incidentally, cause more tickling throats and runny noses than older models because they use such a variety of plastic and textile materials which give off irritating fumes for a few years after they're bought.

Aspirin Overuse

Scientists believe frequent use of aspirin can cause your nose to become blocked. Researchers at the Royal Hallamshire Hospital in Sheffield dosed half of a group of volunteers with aspirin and the other half with vitamin C. Two days later the volunteers swapped doses. Most of the volunteers had runny noses after taking aspirin second, while those given the vitamin second were nasally clear. In general, you may want to avoid aspirin for a cold, unless you are running a temperature.

The Exercise Factor

If you throw yourself around out of doors – jogging, playing football or even dashing for a bus – you'll breathe in more air than usual. As it's one of the nose's jobs to dampen air on its way to the lungs, it will soon start to produce extra moisture to deal with this extra intake of oxygen.

When you stop exerting yourself, the nose continues to secrete more moisture than usual for another 15 minutes or so, so you'll start to drip. Walking to work on a chilly day produces the same effect.

Pregnancy 'Colds'

Many women suffer from runny noses during pregnancy. This is due to changes in their hormones at this time.

Illnesses Similar to Colds

Sore Throat

Though this is a regular symptom of a cold, it can also be caused by bugs unrelated to the cold virus. If the problem lasts longer than a day or two and the nose doesn't start dribbling, you are more likely to have pharyngitis than a cold (*pharynx* is the medical term for the throat). This unpleasant complaint often produces a relentless pain at one point in the throat. It lasts about a week, and only the body's natural defences can cure it. But you can lessen the discomfort with throat sprays, some of which contain a mild anaesthetic, and lozenges. Gargling with salty water will also reduce the pain.

A more severe condition is known as strep throat, after the *streptococcus* bacterium which causes it. This is a nasty complaint, with temperatures rising as high as 104°F, but antibiotics deal with it quickly. Many children carry strep throat bacteria without symptoms, often giving it to classmates. If untreated it can lead to serious complications.

Laryngitis also causes sore throats, this time in that part of the throat known as the *larynx*, where the vocal cords are located. Not surprisingly, the condition often leads to a loss of voice.

Sinusitis

This is a complication of the cold. As it has similar symptoms, it's often hard to know when a cold has gone and sinusitis has taken its place.

One of my minor colds turned to sinusitis lasting three painful months. It started after I had sat too near an electric fire for several hours. I assume the heat expanded the mucus in my nose, forcing it into the sinuses.

These are cavities around the nose within the bones of the face. Like the nose, they are lined with mucus-forming cells. When they become inflamed and filled with mucus, you feel pain above the cheek bones and around the eyes, and you may also run a temperature.

If your previously constantly running nose clears up, but you still can't breathe properly and there is a persistent ache around the eyes, you probably have sinusitis. Nasal sprays can help the sinuses to drain, so allowing the inflammation to heal. In severe cases you will need antibiotics, and sometimes an operation is carried out to drain the cavities.

Colds in Literature

Characters in most of the great 19th century novels rarely had colds. Coughs, mainly of the thin, dry, hacking kind, were reserved for the 'consumptive' – that is, those suffering from, and usually dying of, tuberculosis. The fiction of the period was inclined to death, if at all, with more grandiose complaints, like cholera, malaria, typhoid, and even rabies.

There are, however, a few exceptions.

Ebenezer the Sneezer

Charles Dickens' description of Ebenezer Scrooge's house in *A Christmas Carol* (1843) begins thus: 'Nobody under the table, nobody under the sofa: a small fire in the grate; spoon and basin ready; and the little saucepan of gruel (Scrooge had a cold in his head) upon the hob.' So *that's* why the poor chap wasn't looking forward to the festivities. He probably had an aching throat, a congested nose, a headache and a fever. This groggy state probably forced him to bed early and may even have triggered the very hallucinations on which the whole tale hinges.

The Tactical Cold

Perhaps the best-known chill in 19th century fiction can be found in Jane Austen's *Pride and Prejudice* (1813). The novel hinges on the romantic ambitions of the five Bennet Sisters and the transparent strategies of their mother – a woman

113

'occasionally nervous and invariably silly' – towards securing wealthy husbands for all of them.

The wealthy Bingley family who live three miles away includes an eligible bachelor. Jane, the oldest Bennet girl, is invited to tea.

Mrs Bennet, noting that storm clouds are gathering, tells Jane to pay her social call on horseback rather than take the carriage, since then, if it rained, she would be obliged to stay at the Bingleys' overnight. As it turns out, Jane catches a cold during her ride and has to stay on at the Bingleys' for several days. The duration of the cold not only nurtures the romance of Jane and Mr Bingley but is the means by which the novel's real heroine, Jane's sister Elizabeth, meets her future husband, the seemingly haughty and indubitably wealthy Mr Darcy.

The Curse of the Brontës

That remarkable trio of Victorian novelists, the Brontë sisters, were plagued by tuberculosis. In their draughty old parsonage at Haworth, on the Yorkshire moors, they would have dreaded colds, which make the condition worse. Yet colds are largely absent from their greatest novels. Perhaps the only cold of any consequence – and it is marginal to the main thrust of the story – occurs in Charlotte Brontë's *Villette* (1853): 'Mrs Home had been a very pretty, but a giddy, careless woman who had neglected her child, and disappointed and disheartened her husband. So far from congenial had the union proved, that separation at last ensued. Soon after this event, the lady, having over-exerted herself at a ball, caught cold, took a fever and died after a very short illness.'

This passage reflects a widespread belief at the time: that young ladies leaving balls in fashionable low-neck dresses were much at risk. In Paris alone in the 1820s more than 1,000 ladies were reported to have perished within a year, supposedly from this cause.

An Elementary Cold

Sir Arthur Conan Doyle was an author clever enough to use the ordinary at the beginning of a tale to contrast with the sensational events that would shortly ensue. He uses a common cold for this and also to demonstrate Sherlock Holmes's deductive genius, at the beginning of his story, 'The Stockbroker's Clerk' (1893). Holmes observes to the recently married Watson that he can tell he has been housebound with a summer cold by looking at his slippers.

How can Sherlock infer Watson's snorter from the appearance of his footwear? One side of a slipper is scorched. From this it follows that Watson must have had his feet up by a fire. Why should anyone have a fire in midsummer? He must have been chilled by a cold.

Ghostly Cold

Ghosts, no doubt, can strike terror into those they encounter. But surely even the most credulous would dismiss the possibility of catching a cold from one? Yet in a remarkably chilling modern novel of the supernatural, that is exactly what happens. One of the heroes of *Ghost Story*, by Peter Straub, develops a slight cold in his efforts to hunt down a malignant spirit from his past love-life. His condition steadily worsens as the spirit's situation becomes desperate. The cold is an important part of the story, enhancing the emotional distress and physical fear of its victim.

Rhinoviruses to the Rescue

The common cold is the hero of one of the greatest science fiction novels of all, H.G. Wells' *War of the Worlds* (1898). Martians land in southern England, where they stalk the country in vast machines. Using ray guns, they plunge forward causing wholesale death and desolation.

Just as all seems lost, the machines falter and crash to the ground. The Martians, strangers to infection, have fallen victim to the cold bug. They are killed 'after all man's devices had failed, by the humblest things that God, in His wisdom, has put on earth.' It's a wonderful plot device. It's just that, when I'm in the middle of my winter snorter, no one's going to persuade me that cold viruses are 'humble'.

Mr Pepys's Diary

Samuel Pepys's diary is an astonishingly rich mixture of the everyday and the remarkable, the domestic and the worldly. Colds and other illnesses are noted with the same thoroughness and enthusiasm with which he reports great affairs of state, in which he himself often played a part.

One of his own many colds was brought on, he confesses, when he was disporting lewdly with a lady of title by an open window. On another occasion he returns home to find his wife making tea, which an apothecary, Mr Pelling, has told her is good for her cold and 'defluxions' (runny nose).

The Booze Cure

In the 15th century a common treatment for colds was to plunge a red-hot poker into a mug of stout, to which ginger was added. It was drunk, while still warm, by adults and children alike. Later, in wealthier households, whisky in hot water with honey was popular, as was mulled wine.

Those with too little faith in their fellow men have suggested that these delightful tipples might be taken more for their taste than their curative properties. Hitherto, the riposte to such a *canard* was that having something pleasant to drink when one was feeling groggy should not be condemned. But now, it seems, there is a more positive line of argument: it really does look as though a little tipple will help a sniffle.

Shortly before it closed, the Cold Research Centre carried out a three-year study into the effects of alcohol on the common cold. They were helped by 400 volunteers, aged from 18 to 50. The lucky 200 were each given a pint and a half of beer or three glasses of wine per day, while the other 200 were allowed no alcohol at all. But all 400 had viruses stuffed up their noses.

It was found that only 30 out of the 200 drinkers suffered symptoms, while nearly half the abstainers developed the usual miseries. The study also indicated that the protection given by the alcohol is reliable only if you drink, albeit moderately, every day.

This suggests that people who like going to the pub are three times less likely to catch colds than those who don't.

Against this must be set the undoubted possibility that you will encounter many more cold viruses at the pub than at home.

Just a glass of beer or spirits, or two glasses of wine should be enough to keep bugs at bay. More alcohol may be more effective, but it's not worth trying for two good reasons: a hangover is often as bad as a cold; and too much of the hard stuff makes your nose run.

Booze v. Bugs

The clue to the role of alcohol lies in the fact that some of the imbibers in the Wiltshire experiments were shown by blood tests to have cold viruses at work in their systems. Clinically speaking they had colds, but there were no runny noses, raspy throats, coughs or sneezes. This suggests that alcohol strikes not at the viruses but at the symptoms.

As we've seen, the human body has a mechanism for dealing with inflammation of the tissues. In the case of nasal passages swollen by a cold, it causes the nose to run and the eyes to stream. It's possible that alcohol blocks the process. Other possibilities are that a little boozing stimulates the immune system or that alcohol acts directly on mucus, drying it up.

The cheapest way to research the question yourself is to keep an eye on the office drunk and see whether he or she gets as many colds as you do.

The Hunt Is On

Fame, fortune, and a great advance in human welfare may reward the researchers all over the world who are engaged in a ceaseless search to find a total cure for the common cold. Some lines of inquiry have proved more promising than others. Here are some of the more unusual quests for success.

The Kakko Cure

Kakko is a herb that has been used in Chinese medicine for centuries and is now being studied by Japanese virologists as a possible cold cure.

A drug, known as RO-09-0415, was extracted from the Kakko plant by a team working for Nippon Roche, the Tokyo arm of the multinational pharmaceutical company. They synthesized chemicals with molecular structures similar to extractions from the herb. These were found to kill 98% of rhinoviruses in five minutes.

But experiments in the laboratory are not the same as trials on humans. And although the new drug is believed not to have any serious side effects, it may not be available from your chemist for some while, if at all.

The Steam Box

A joint French-Israeli project has developed a machine called the Rhinotherm, which pumps out moist air heated to 41.5°C

(107°F). It's been shown that when this hot air is inhaled, many cold viruses are obliterated.

Interferon

High hopes were held for this anti-viral agent as a cure for colds. It's already made in small amounts by our own cells when they're under attack, but not in quantities large enough to have a noticeable effect.

Interferon from other sources could be applied up our noses, but it is extremely expensive as it can be obtained only in very small quantities from other animals, including pigs and horses.

Though interferon makes short work of cold viruses, it has two serious disadvantages: you need to take it *before* any symptoms show; and it has side effects rather like the symptoms of a cold.

Why Lumberjacks are OK

A little boy living by the forests of Norway noticed that lumberjacks never blew their noses. He grew up to be a chemistry student at Oslo University, and later qualified as a doctor of biochemistry after training at the University of Minnesota.

Olav Braenden then returned to study the woodcutters, who lived in huts with open hearths and holes in the roof. Unsurprisingly, they breathed in a great deal of woodsmoke. Braenden wondered if this helped to ward off colds.

His research took him to the World Health Organisation in Geneva, and eventually he was able to isolate the chemicals in smoke known as polyphenols.

The Norwegian Air Force dosed 300 recruits with Braenden's new anti-cold drug in the form of nose drops. A success rate of over 80 per cent was reported. It is believed that polyphenols, if taken with vitamins B and C, starve the lining of the nose of oxygen, so inhibiting the cold viruses.

The Sniffer and the Rose

Aromatherapists, who use the essential oils of plants on their patients, have long held that the scents of flowers have antiseptic qualities. A study by West German scientists supports this claim – at least in the case of roses.

After setting down vases of roses in the same room as cold-ridden volunteers, the boffins spotted a big improvement in their breathing. Those with headaches also started feeling better. Additionally rose oil is thought to be good for the nerves, calming anxiety and depression – both conditions which aggravate colds.

Relax, You Won't Catch a Cold

The conviction that a negative state of mind can encourage colds has been with us a long time. It was given extra weight when researchers at the University of Pittsburgh sifted material assembled at the Common Cold Research Centre in Wiltshire. The Americans processed the records of 20,000 voluteers collected since the end of the war, and there was no doubt about it: unhappy or worried people are more prone to develop colds than happy ones.

The Role of Stress

The key to the above discovery is stress: surveys show it doubles the risk of colds. Those moving house, changing jobs, having a baby, or appearing in court are easy targets. Entertainers come down with serious colds on opening night. Exam-takers struggle through their ordeal with damp handkerchiefs at their sides. Many politicians go into the general election campaigns so affected by colds they can hardly speak.

The consequence is that we often end up with a debilitating and unsightly affliction just when we need to look and feel our best. But that's not the end of it: that well-known double act, stress and tension (not quite the same thing) not only trigger colds – they prolong the symptoms and make them feel worse.

How our state of mind affects what sounds like a

straightforward physical change in our noses is still not clear. There must be a relationship between our immunity mechanism and psychological tensions in the brain.

Researchers are excited by that link and will continue to study what are called the psychosomatic mechanisms involved in cold infections. Stress, incidentally, is suspected of aggravating other, more serious maladies, including cancer and AIDS.

Stress and Delayed Symptoms

A rather strange connection between stress and the cold is what is called the delaying factor. Often people show no sign of a runny nose until *after* their anxiety and its cause have disappeared. This is why many unfortunate people start a cold at the same time as a summer holiday or the week they retire.

There may be an age-old explanation for this. Anthropologists say that when our caveman ancestors were fighting marauding sabre-tooth tigers, they couldn't afford to be weakened by an infection. So bodily defences tried that bit harder, and collapsed only when danger had passed.

The Happy Cold

Happiness is a form of excitement related to stress, and giving your heart to someone can cause a cold. I can think of at least two well-known song lyrics which link respiratory infection with falling in love. A bout of the sniffles can also follow a wedding, passing an exam or winning the pools.

The Executive Cold

The fact that cold symptoms often strike after a period of intense work has led to the myth that top executives can put off their colds until the week-end or their holidays. It does not mean, however, that they are miracle workers; it's just the post-stress syndrome at work again.

*Ah! I was about to ask what day of the week
you usually catch cold?*

The inventor of Parkinson's Law ('Work expands to fill the time available for its completion') enters the story here. C. Northcote Parkinson once said interviewers should always ask candidates for top jobs on what day of the week they caught the most colds. Only if the answer was Friday night, rather than earlier in the week, should they get the post.

There is however scientific evidence that people who are in secure jobs at the top of the tree get fewer colds than colleagues further down the ladder. Being resentful at a lack of promotion, or in constant fear of redundancy, makes you twice as likely to develop a cold as the company director who has already made it to the top.

Why Common Colds Are Booming

Colds have developed and expanded in scope as society has evolved. In pre-Roman Britain communities were small and more isolated, and their members often spent their whole lives without meeting more than a few strangers from outside the settlement. Colds introduced into such communities would flare up quickly but would soon run their course, and the villagers might go many years before they encountered a different cold virus. For this reason, the proliferation of viruses into many different strains would have been gradual. Today, as we have seen, there are about 300 strains; and because of our predominantly urban way of life, the number is increasing all the time.

Danger in the Air

A virus developed on another continent would once have travelled extremely slowly to reach Britain, and people had time to build up immunity as it moved from nose to nose. In the old days, a bug boarding a ship in India or Australia, would have gone round the crew and passengers and would probably have become spent by the time it arrived in England.

Today a virus on a jumbo jet arrives here in a few hours. Its carrier might just be starting a cold when he lands, so he will be at his most infectious stage. No one on these shores will have immunity against this foreign strain, and it will sweep through the population.

A Weak-counter Attack

Thanks to medical advances, the UK population is getting older. As we've seen, elderly people get fewer colds. And if you haven't got a cold you can't pass it on.

Ironically, what some people regard as less desirable changes in modern life are limiting the spread of colds. This applies to:

* Film fans who hire videos rather than go to cinemas.
* Children who play solitary computer games rather than hide-and-seek with other children.
* Music lovers who buy CDs rather than go to live concerts.
* Commuters who use cars rather than bikes or public transport.

Even so, the freedom from infection for any of these groups will be short-lived. Their immunity systems will get out of practice, so when they do meet viruses the symptoms will be worse.

Silver Linings

This wasn't an easy chapter for a dyed-in-the-wool cold-hater like me. But it must be conceded that, just like everything else, the common cold is not *all* bad.

To anyone in the throes of a scorching throat, a splitting cranium, and raw nose like an outlet pipe this is going to sound all very unlikely but, in the hope of making you feel a little better, let me list some of the advantages of acute coryza.

A Temporary Cure for Workaholics

A cold slows people down. This may not seem like a benefit for your lazy husband, indolent teenage daughter or work-shy employee but, in the case of workaholics with high blood pressure, it can save lives. Even those high-flyers, who refuse to let a watery nose stop them in their tracks, are pulled up despite themselves.

The brain becomes rather fuzzy; it doesn't work as fast. And those aching muscles stop you galloping around all over the place. In the later stages, the voice stops working properly so you're less inclined to use it. Try as you may to maintain your pace, physically you just can't.

In the long term, therefore, your general health will improve as well as your career.

As a Useful Indicator of Poor Health

Some alternative medics will tell you that a cold isn't an illness but a cure. What they mean is that you won't contract one unless you are already under par. Reacting badly to the virus means your defence mechanism has been too fragile to repel it.

If, therefore, you topple with a series of colds, your body needs an overhaul. You should, for instance, eat fewer empty calories, sleep more, do less work and try to relax.

Without cold viruses you might never realize your immunity is run down, thus making you easy prey to more serious illnesses. Another good reason, perhaps, why nature doesn't want us to find an instant cure.

Keeping Unemployment Figures Down

More days are lost to industry through colds than to any other disease. And that includes backache, arthritis, hangovers and flu.

If all those suffering from colds were at work, most employers would need a smaller staff. Worldwide, the common cold gives millions more people the opportunity to work. Also, the drugs industry employs hundreds of thousands of people making powders, potions, pills, rubs, syrups and nose sprays, and the paper-tissue industry thrives.

As people languish in bed or lie supine on the sofa, they still need something to do. The sales of videos, books, newspapers, jigsaws, wire puzzles and hot-water bottles are all improved by colds. I would say that it's certain that many firms will go bust the day the cure is found.

Preventing Base Designs

Among the ambitions inhibited by colds are the evil ones. And, as you saw in the chapter on famous historical colds, they have been known to thwart the cruel designs of

dictators. The best known example is Napoleon's snorter which put him off during the Battle of Borodino, saving Russia from occupation.

A Jolly Good Excuse

Think how many boring or arduous appointments you would have kept if you hadn't been struck down. As a child, you would have had many more Latin periods, games sessions and piano lessons to put up with. And, as an adult, you would have visited more unpleasant relatives, done more work in the garden or been dragged off to more dreary parties...

Foreign embassies all use the 'diplomatic cold'. Its most useful application is in avoiding an arranged official visit at a politically embarrassing moment. For example, a member of the royal family is booked to open a new dam in Dubiland. Between the time of accepting the invitation and the date of the visit, an 'international incident' arises: Dubiland suddenly invades a neighbour. If the visit goes ahead, it would seem like an endorsement of the hostile action towards the neighbouring country, with which we have healthy trade connections. But, to refuse to make the official visit will offend and could even mean war. So an announcement is made that, unfortunately, the important visitor has a cold and can't go. Both sides know that this cold doesn't actually exist but diplomatic face is saved.

My Lords, Ladies and Gentlemen

Wheezes and sneezes that trouble others can be especially welcome on social occasions. I'm thinking mainly of those barren speeches we're all forced to listen to now and then. Fortunately, the season for this kind of junket starts in October and November when the viruses are most rampant. And a combination of blocked nose, hacking cough and fragile voice can curtail the most persistent of after-dinner bores. Not only that, but colds interfere with memory, making it harder for an afflicted speaker to recall exactly

Let's get out of here!

what he's talking about.

So next time you see an after-dinner orator flounder and sit down in a hurry, he might well be telling the truth when he blames 'something he was taking for the cold', and not an excess of drink.

Unimaginative speakers also blight our lives from cradle to grave, from school speech days and weddings to retirement parties and funeral addresses. Think how many tortured hours you've been spared by the humble cold!

Little Green Men

Are cold viruses meant to protect us from catastrophe in the future? Out there in the inky universe, there may be green eyes looking enviously at Earth. If so where are they? Why haven't they attacked?

Could it be that the aliens have no lymph glands, bone marrow, white cells, T-cells or antibodies to protect them from the humble rhinovirus and his friends. If so, to arrive anywhere on this planet would be fatal. As far as space invaders are concerned, the common cold may have turned us into the fabled Forbidden Planet.

Cold Facts

Keep Smiling

A large Anglo-American study found that introverts have to put up with worse symptoms than extroverts from the same cold virus. This is not merely because introspective people worry more about their symptoms: they really *do* suffer more. One possible explanation is that an inward-looking, self-absorbed personality has an inhibiting effect on the body's immune system.

Old Versus New

United States servicemen billeted in old wartime huts have been found to have only half as many colds as their comrades in modern buildings. It's believed that draughts blowing through cracks in the woodwork and ill-fitting doors keep the air fresh.

In newer buildings stale, infected air circulates from person to person. Some air-conditioning systems also send viruses round and round again.

Cold War of the Sexes

More women catch colds than men. True, most mothers spend more time with cold-attracting toddlers than do the fathers. On the other hand, it's known that little girls catch more colds than boys. So it seems that women are physically more susceptible. By way of compensation, men get worse colds than women – or is it simply that men whinge more loudly?

It's thought that women's hormonal cycles prepare their bodies for changes. When a cold virus attacks a man, it's a bigger shock to his system. But a woman's body is more used to upsets, and it is better able to accommodate the invader. A study carried out in Chicago showed that women are more likely to get a cold during the third week of their menstrual cycle, and that they were most likely to succumb if the room temperature was lower than normal.

A Running Cold

Biologists believe that athletes, especially runners, have more colds than most people. Although they're obviously fitter than the rest of us, it's likely that the stress of competing undermines their immunity. Body-builders are even more prone to colds, as most of their energy reserves go into enlarging their muscles, rather than strengthening the body's defence system.

The Bedside Manner

One research project has found a causal link between the doctor's attitude and the condition of patients with coughs and sneezes. If the GP is friendly and sympathetic, the cold clears up faster than if he's rude, dismissive or merely indifferent.

Colds and Time Off

A survey by British employment agency Alfred Marks showed that 96 out of 100 companies listed colds and flu as the main reason why employees take time off work. Backache came a poor second. In Britain alone, 100 million working days are lost annually through illness. It was once estimated that Americans have up to 1000 million colds and bouts of flu every year.

Hankie History

Before the invention of handkerchiefs, most people wiped their nose on their sleeves. They were introduced from China in the 15th century, when French sailors returned with linen coverings on their heads. They called them *couvrechefs* (head-covers). In Britain this was anglicized as kerchiefs. They were quickly adopted by women.

They were later carried by men and women as a fashion accessory, and in Britain became known as handkerchiefs. Trivia question: who is said to have first suggested that handkerchiefs be used to mop up colds? Answer: Desiderius Erasmus (1466–1536), the great Dutch humanist philosopher.

Smokers and Colds

Smokers imperil their health in many ways, but controlled tests show they're no more likely to develop colds than non-smokers. However, smokers can expect the symptoms to last longer: any irritants which are breathed in when viruses are in control stimulate the nasal flow.

Animal Colds

Some animals other than man catch colds, including apes such as chimpanzees, gorillas, gibbons and orang-utans. Other primates, such as monkeys, don't get colds, but horses, young cattle, and cats do share the affliction with us. Rabbits, rats, guinea pigs and mice get snuffly noses; but these aren't true colds because bacteria, not viruses, are responsible.

Concert Coughs

The Hallé Orchestra once took the offensive against cold sufferers who attended a performance of Beethoven's Ninth Symphony. Everyone arriving at the Free Trade Hall in

Manchester was handed a herbal lozenge after earlier concerts had been disrupted by heavy and continuous coughing.

Tests had been carried out on six sweets to find one which could be unwrapped more quietly than the others. A Swiss lozenge in greased paper was selected.

Jailhouse Cough

People with colds faced extra misery in the United States in 1919: they could be thrown into jail. At that time it was an offence to sneeze in public. Actually, it was influenza sufferers the authorities were trying to keep off the streets. The world was gripped by a flu epidemic which eventually killed 20 million. Cold and hay-fever sufferers were locked up like the rest.

A Cold Sort of Love

Derek and Yvonne Russ of Kingskerswell, Devon, spent their honeymoon trying to catch a cold. Their bridal suite was a spartan research room at the Cold Research Centre in Wiltshire.

After having cold viruses put up their noses, they were put into isolation. Food was left outside their door, together with flowers and a bottle of wine.

Derek, a 26-year-old wages clerk, later said: 'We really wanted to go to Israel, but couldn't afford it'. Neither of them caught a cold during their 10-day stay.

The Cat and the Cold

An old superstition says that if your black cat sneezes once it's a lucky sign, but if it sneezes thrice your entire family will catch colds.

I'll Try and Read That Again

TV and radio broadcasters put up with a lot of real stinkers. Their resistance tends to be low because of their anti-social working hours: the body's not happy at their reading the news at two o'clock on Sunday morning. They also handle scripts, notes and news flashes that will previously have been handled by producers and sub-editors, any one of whom could be harbouring rhinoviruses. Finally they may be talking to reporters who have flown in from distant parts of the world and may be carrying a variety of cold viruses new to this country.

The Art of Nose Blowing

When blowing your nose, don't just enfold it willy nilly in a handkerchief. The correct way is to press on one side of the nose with your hankie, so that you expel mucus from the nostril on the other side. Then you reverse the process.

Some people accidentally block both nostrils by pinching the nose as they blow. This can lead to liquid being forced upwards into the ear, and it is possible to rupture the eardrum in this way.

Epilogue

In *Confessions of an English Opium-Eater* (1821) Thomas De Quincey tells us 'It is remarkable that during the whole period of years through which I had taken opium, I had never once caught cold, nor even the slightest cough.' But when he eventually gave up the drug: 'Now a violent cold attacked me, and a cough soon after.'

Long years of drug abuse, however, is not the answer. What the world needs now is a new anti-viral drug that will banish the age-old nuisance once and for all. Only when we get an effective cold-destroying drug will the world be saved from all those serious diseases started by colds, from millions of lost days at work, from the huge amounts of money spent on symptom-relievers, and from countless weeks of human misery.

Some cynics, however, are asking whether a total cure will make much initial difference. When an anti-cold medicine comes on the market there are likely to be two snags. First, it is bound to be expensive to reflect all the years and investment put into the quest so far. It's even possible that the National Health Service would not want to offer it on prescription, as treating such a common ailment would cost billions. Second, like nearly all drugs, it will have side effects.

The question will be: is it worth paying a lot and risking those side effects for an illness which only lasts a week and doesn't put you completely out of action? Most people, I fancy, will answer 'Yes.'